745.5   1977142

Layman, Teresa.

Gingerbread: things to
make and bake

P9-CAN-719

OCT 2 5 2011

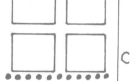

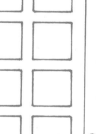

EMPORIA PUBLIC
LIBRARY

In Memory
Of
Coralea Cranz

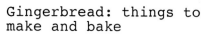

GINGERBREAD
THINGS TO MAKE AND BAKE

GINGERBREAD
Things to Make and Bake

The Quilting Bee

By Teresa Layman and Barbara Morgenroth
Photography by Randy O'Rourke
Harry N. Abrams, Inc., Publishers

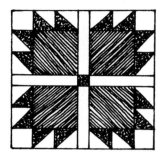

EDITOR: Ellen Rosefsky
DESIGNER: Darilyn Lowe Carnes

Library of Congress Cataloging-in-Publication Data

Layman, Teresa.
    Gingerbread : things to make and bake / by Teresa Layman and
Barbara Morgenroth ; photography by Randy O'Rourke.
        p.   cm.
    Includes bibliographical references and index.
    ISBN 0–8109–3367–5
    1. Gingerbread.   2. Handicraft.   I. Morgenroth, Barbara.
II. Title.
TX771.L38   1992   91–42923
641.8′653—dc20   CIP

Copyright © 1992 Teresa Layman and Barbara Morgenroth
Photographs copyright © 1992 Harry N. Abrams, Inc.

Published in 1992 by Harry N. Abrams, Incorporated, New York
A Times Mirror Company
All rights reserved. No part of the contents of this book may
be reproduced without the written permission of the publisher

Printed and bound in Japan

Contents

Introduction

WHEN HANSEL AND GRETEL walked through the dark and dangerous forest, they came upon a house made of gingerbread. This folktale was first told in eighteenth-century Germany, when ginger and gingerbread were well over two thousand years old. The brothers Grimm's retelling of this already popular tale elevated the notion of a gingerbread house and made it familiar to both the European and American audiences.

Ginger is a spice indigenous to Indo-Malaysia. The ginger root was and still is believed to have medicinal properties, useful in soothing an upset stomach or preventing a cold. As early as 2000 B.C. wealthy Grecian families sailed to the Isle of Rhodes for these spiced honey cakes.

In the eleventh century, pilgrims and soldiers returned home from the Crusades and introduced ginger to the Europeans, along with other spices and treasures. Almost instantly the English created a therapeutic ginger candy. Two hundred years later, bread crumbs were added to the mixture and gingerbread was born. Geoffrey Chaucer wrote in *Sir Thopas* in 1386, "They sette hym Roial spicerye And gyngebreed" ("They gave him royal spices and gingerbread").

Gingerbread is a honey spice dough that does not contain nuts or fruits. Here is a recipe for gingerbread from the fourteenth century:

> *"To make gingerbread. Take a good honey & clarify it on the fire, & take fair white bread & grate it, & cast it into the boiling honey, & stir it well together fast with a slice so that it does not burn to the pot. & then take it down and put therein ginger, long pepper & saunders, & temper it up with thine hands; & then put them into a flat box & strew thereon sugar, & pick therein cloves round about by the edge and in the middle, if it please you, & ..." (translated by David Friedman and Betty Cook, from* Curye on Inglysch, *ed. Constance B. Hieatt and Sharon Butler, Early English Text Society, 1985, p. 154)*

This modern version of the old English text makes the original recipe easier to understand but not to duplicate in the kitchen.

In the Middle Ages, the popularity of ginger increased. Medieval ladies presented gingerbread cakes to their favored knights, often painted with colored sugars or embossed to create a leather-like appearance. The fleur-de-lis was a popular shape as well as that of Saint Nicholas, the patron saint of marriageable young women and men. Other shapes were used as talismans: the heart was used to ward off evil, rabbits as a symbol of fertility, and stags for virility.

While spices were very expensive for most Europeans, this was not the case for Germans living near Nuremberg, the center of the spice trade. They regarded gingerbread so highly that craft unions specialized in baking intricate representations of the aristocratic life-style. Using carved wooden molds, fabricated by a separate union, various shapes such as animals, fish, flowers, and biblical scenes were stamped out. To further enhance these elaborate creations, often weighing over a hundred pounds, gold leaf was used for decoration. Soon the expression "To take the gilt off the gingerbread" came into usage, meaning to deprive something of its attractive qualities.

During the fourteenth century it was possible to find recipes for pastry castles complete with four corner towers and one larger embattlement in the center of the building. It is believed that the creation of structural gingerbread (dough that is baked so that it is sturdy enough to be used as support members) came into use in the early part of the eighteenth century.

Gingerbread is listed as *gingibretum* in medieval Latin pharmaceutical manuals and in 1573 was referred to as a comfort for the stomach when used as either a cake or a paste. But gingerbread from this time onward also became widely accepted as a plain cake made with treacle (a syrup of refined sugar) and flavored with a good amount of ginger. The expression "cake and gingerbread" was often used in sixteenth-century England to describe something easy and pleasant. For many years, the use of ginger was limited by both its expense and its scarcity, causing it to be reserved for special occasions. Small gingerbread cookies known as snaps or buttons could be found on feast days and at street fairs in England.

In the late-sixteenth-century English court of Queen Elizabeth I, where ginger had long been held in high esteem, guests were presented with gingerbread fancies, each with a portrait of that person. In Nuremberg, December brought the *Christkindlmarkt* (child of Christ market) where all the Christmas specialties were purchased. Here the holiday decorations, meats, pastries, and sausages were displayed, as well as the colorfully iced and decorated *Lebkuchen* (cake for the living), a traditional German cake baked on a wafer, made of ginger and other spices.

It took the discovery of the New World and the introduction of molasses to Europe in the seventeenth century to create the gingerbread we are familiar with, that is, cakelike without bread crumbs. It was then not reserved only for royalty and the wealthy but available to everyone.

During the Victorian era, when life turned away from the streets, markets, fairs, and public celebrations were relegated to the past and people became more home oriented. This was when gingerbread houses became more popular in America. As Christmas trees grew more opulent and lavish with glass ornaments, candles, and garlands, so did gingerbread houses. Competitions still exist to determine who can build the most elaborate structure; church groups in Pennsylvania and Connecticut fill auditoriums with every imaginable edifice provided it is entirely edible.

Today most American-made gingerbread is seasonal and relegated to simplified gingerbread men and women, whereas in Holland and Belgium intricate figures are made during the celebration of Saint Nicholas Day. In Scandinavia, pig-shaped cookies announce the Christmas season to children.

In Germany, too, the heritage of gingerbread houses continues to present times. Native Germans still talk about their village being repre-sented in gingerbread; each family would bring a model of their home to a central location where the village was recreated in miniature. Others speak of the tradition of building the houses and waiting until New Year's Day, when the children of the household would take small mallets to break their gingerbread house apart. Then they would eat the pieces to usher in the new year.

Limited solely by our imaginations as to what we can create with gingerbread, this book is meant as an introduction to house building. If you are a novice in making gingerbread structures, the easiest projects are the Sweet Shop, the Woodsman's Cabin, the Ski Chalet, and the ornaments. The accessories are all interchangeable; you can ice the walls of any struc-ture to add color or to personalize it. If you feel more daring, use the basics provided here and design your own house, or make a replica of your cottage, your house, or your castle. It is all part of the tradition.

Gingerbread Supply List

Tools and Materials

electric mixer
mixing bowls
small bowls for mixing icing colors
wooden spoon
rolling pin
1 or 2 baking sheets
baking parchment
wire rack (rectangular, at least the size of your baking sheet)
icing spatula
thin blade knife
windowpane cookie cutters (optional)
patterns (given for each building)
manila file folders or oak tag board
X-acto® or craft knife
pencil
ruler

scissors
tracing paper
icing bags and couplers
icing tips: #2, #4, #6 writing, #67 leaf, #14 star
toothpicks
plywood board (for size refer to specific house instructions)
brown paper
masking tape
decorative ribbon or lace
tweezers
wire (for Quilt Shop only)
Styrofoam®1/2" thick (for Row Houses and Church)
1/4" foam core board (for Mill only)
drill and drill bit the diameter of your candy sticks (for Row Houses, Sweet Shop)
hammer to pulverize hard candies (for Church only)
silica gel in bags for storage (optional)

Candies and Decorations

ROOFING MATERIALS

Necco® candy wafers
whole pecans
sliced almonds
cinnamon gum (Big Red®)
licorice gum (Black Jack®)
Smarties®
Golden Grahams® cereal
Triscuit Bits®
Triscuits®
Keebler® Sun-toasted Wheats
Bran Chex® cereal

FENCING MATERIALS

long pretzel sticks (split rail fence)
piped icing (picket or iron fence)

candy pebbles (stone wall)
snack pretzels

WALKWAYS

broken Necco® candy wafers (slate or stone)
chocolate sprinkles
PEZ® candies
licorice gum (Black Jack®)

CHIMNEYS

mocha beans
caramels and chocolate caramels
broken Necco® candy wafers (black, brown, and purple)
PEZ® candies

Photograph courtesy Teresa Layman

MISCELLANEOUS

*sugar sequins (little flowers or snowflakes also called
snowflake DÉCORS by McCormick & Co.)
cinnamon hearts (small)
cinnamon Red Hots® (small and round)
cherry hearts (large) (SPREE®)
silver dragées
colored nonpareils
sanding sugar (coarse sugar)
green sugar crystals
cocoa powder
candy canes and sticks (regular size and jumbo)
green jelly spearmint leaves
red gumdrops
yellow jelly candies (BRACH®'s Fruit Bunch®) for
lamp posts
Tootsie Rolls®
pretzel rods
sugar cones (small and large)
marzipan
shredded coconut
royal icing
food coloring (liquid, paste, and powder)*

Photograph courtesy Teresa Layman

Gingerbread Dough Recipe (1 Batch)

6 3/4 cups flour
1 tablespoon cinnamon
1 1/2 teaspoons ginger
1/2 teaspoon salt
1 1/2 cups light corn syrup*
1 1/4 cups packed light brown sugar*
1 cup margarine

Preheat oven to 350 degrees. Stir the dry ingredients together in a large bowl.

Combine light corn syrup, light brown sugar, and margarine in a 2-quart saucepan. Stir constantly over medium heat until margarine is melted.

Stir the liquid into the flour mixture. Mix well using hands to mix as dough becomes stiff. Chill the dough until it is easy to handle. Roll the dough out to a 1/8" thickness on parchment paper. Using the patterns provided, cut into the required shapes. Bake for 12 to 15 minutes or until golden brown. Check for air bubbles during baking and poke them with a sharp knife or a toothpick. When baking is done, slide the parchment with the hot cookies onto a large cooling rack. Make sure all pieces lie flat.

*NOTE: Dark corn syrup or dark brown sugar may be substituted and will result in darker dough.

Royal Icing Recipe

1-pound box powdered sugar
3 egg whites at room temperature
1/8 teaspoon cream of tartar

Sift the entire pound of sugar to remove all lumps. Place egg whites in mixer bowl. Add sugar and cream of tartar to whites while stirring. When all the sugar is incorporated, turn mixer on high and beat mixture until thick and *very* white. Mixture will hold a peak. This process should take 5 to 7 minutes. When finished, cover icing tightly with a damp cloth or plastic wrap as it dries very quickly and will form a crust.

To tint icing, use a small amount of color at a time. Paste food colors will not change the consistency of the icing as liquid colorings will. You only need to add a small amount to make a pastel color. For a quarter cup of icing, dip the tip of a toothpick into the color and then into the icing. Stir well. If you desire more color, dip again, gradually. For strong colors such as red, royal blue, and dark purple, you will need 1/8 teaspoon to 1/4 cup icing. Add more or less as you desire.

NOTE: If you plan to make several colors as you will for ornaments, a muffin tin makes a handy palette.

General Instructions

I T IS WISE TO have all tools, decorations, dough, and icing (check against the supply list on page 10) set out in an orderly fashion to insure a speedy creation of your building. Also, read through all of the general directions and those directions for the building you have chosen before beginning, to give you a better understanding of what to expect.

Your first step should be to transfer the patterns onto a heavy stock paper. Manila file folders or oak tag work well for this purpose. *All the patterns provided in this book are actual size.* As you cut out the patterns, remember to cut out the doors and windows, which can easily be done with an X-acto® or craft knife. Make sure you have the required number of pieces to complete each building. It is possible to be in the process of adding the last wall and realize you never cut it out hours earlier.

While you may think a rainy, wet day is the best time to tackle a gingerbread project, it is the worst; try to avoid baking in any kind of humid weather. Structural gingerbread needs to be dry and rigid. If it absorbs too much moisture in the air, the walls tend to sag. Royal icing, on the other hand, favors more humid conditions; lack of moisture causes the icing to crack and break.

These two requirements can present problems of storage in many areas of the country. In the Northwest, for example, it is possible to store a gingerbread house from one year to the next, while in the Northeast, prolonging the life of a project beyond four weeks can be difficult. To preserve your structures, you can try using polyurethane sprays, but we have not found anything that satisfactorily prolongs the life expectancy of gingerbread when the weather is against you. Our best advice for storing a project is to put it in an airtight container and pack it with several bags of silica gel.

Once you have decided upon your project and have all the supplies at hand, follow these step-by-step instructions to create each building:

1. Transfer pattern to manila file folders or oak tag by using tracing paper or by measuring.
2. Cut out and label all pattern pieces.
3. Make gingerbread dough and chill as required.

4. Assemble necessary items for building and decorating your chosen structure according to list given.

5. For the base, cover a piece of plywood board with brown paper, using masking tape to hold it in place (size of board given in each supply list).

6. Roll the gingerbread dough to a thickness of 1/8" on parchment paper. Using the patterns provided, cut out the required shapes. Cut out all windows using a very sharp, thin-bladed knife or window cutter (see source list). Be sure to keep your cutting utensil clean as bits of dough can build up and create ragged cuts. Bake at 350 degrees for 12 to 15 minutes or until golden brown. While baking, prick air bubbles with a toothpick or bamboo skewer.

7. To cool, slide the parchment with hot gingerbread onto a large wire rack. Make sure all pieces lie flat.

8. When cool, place pieces in a single layer on a towel. Do not stack them as the weight will break the bottom pieces.

9. Make required batch of royal icing.

10. Fill a pastry bag with royal icing and fit it with a #6 writing tip.

11. Decide where your house will sit on the base board. Decide where the main walls will be and lay them face down on the board (see fig. 1).

12. Pipe a wide line of icing on the board corresponding to the bottoms of the side and front walls.

13. Pipe a line of icing on the back side of the front wall, along both edges where the side walls will attach.

14. Simultaneously affix these sections to the base board and to each other at a 90° angle.

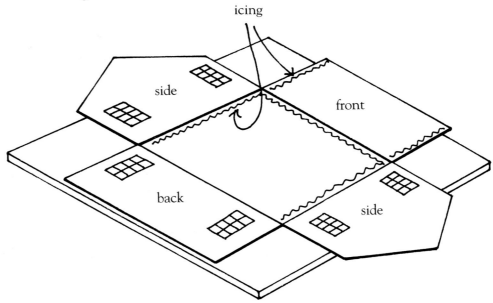

fig. 1 HOUSE PIECES FLAT WITH ICING PLACEMENT

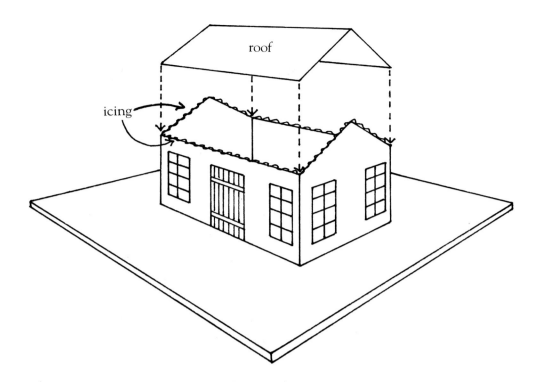

fig. 2 HOUSE PIECES WITH WALLS STANDING, WITH ICING AND ROOF PLACEMENT

15. Attach the back wall in the same manner. If the building you are constructing has more than four walls, work your way around until all walls are standing (see fig. 2).

16. Let set until firm.

ROOF

Roofs are all constructed in a similar fashion whether it is a two-piece roof or one with several sections.

1. For the houses with a two-piece roof, pipe icing around all upper edges of walls.

2. Set on roof pieces leaving desired overhang towards front and sides of building. Hold in place approximately 1 minute so icing has a chance to set.

3. Pipe a line of icing along the ridgepole of roof.

4. For buildings with more than two roof sections, attach the largest pieces first as they will be the base for the smaller pieces.

5. Attach smaller pieces.

6. With the house standing, let set about 1 hour.

Shingles

When applying shingles to the roof, the first row is always at the bottom edge of the roof.

1. Run a line of icing using a #4 pastry tip along the eaves 1/4" from the edge. Using your desired roofing material, prepared in advance if need be, attach shingles in a straight line to make the first row.

2. For second row, cut or break one shingle in half vertically. Begin with this shingle (this offsets the rows so rain will not get into the building) and continue as before.

3. Completely cover the roof.

NOTE: Some roofing materials, such as pecan halves or Smarties®, are too thick to overlap so they are simply fixed to the roof in rows.

CHOCOLATE SHINGLES

1. Melt 18 ounces of chocolate chips and spread onto a thin layer in a parchment-lined cookie sheet. Refrigerate 5 minutes.

2. Cut into 1" squares and freeze for about 10 minutes until solid.

3. Attach to roof with icing.

NOTE: You may need to return the pan to the freezer periodically as the shingles become soft while you work with them.

Chimney

There are many candies to use for masonry. Some favorites are chocolate mocha beans, PEZ® candies, caramels (both light and dark), and broken Necco® candy wafers in black, brown, and purple.

CARAMEL CHIMNEY

1. With a sharp knife, cut several caramels into brick shapes (usually three slices per caramel).

2. Following the pattern for chimney placement, pipe the lines onto the side of the house for a chimney outline. You will build the chimney inside these lines.

3. Pipe the bottom row of icing and set on two or three bricks. Pipe the next row of icing and add the next row of bricks, but offset them as you did on the roof shingles. You will find it necessary to cut some of the bricks in half for the end pieces.

4. Continue the pattern up until the chimney reaches the eaves. At this point use whole caramels and cut one caramel on an angle. Place this one on top of the roof as an extension of the chimney. Proceed to build the chimney to a height of about four caramels with icing between each one.

5. Let each layer dry a bit before continuing on to the next.

6. The top layer of bricks is made from one flattened caramel with lines scored in it. Half of a cotton ball can be used for smoke.

NECCO® CANDY WAFER CHIMNEY

1. Following the pattern for chimney placement, pipe the lines onto the side of the house for a chimney outline. You will build the chimney inside these lines.

2. Prepare your Necco® candy wafers by separating the black, brown, and purple wafers from the rest. Break the dark colors into odd shapes.

3. Starting at the bottom of the chimney, between the guidelines, pipe several rows of icing with a #4 pastry tip so that you cover about 2".

4. Set the broken Necco® candy wafers into the icing, working the pieces together as you would a jigsaw puzzle. Carefully wipe away any excess icing with your finger.

5. Continue up the chimney in this manner until you reach the top of the wall.

6. At this point use whole caramels and cut one caramel on an angle. Place this one on top of the roof as an extension of the chimney. Proceed to build the chimney up to a height of about four caramels with icing between each one. Let dry.

7. Cover the caramels in "stonework" as you did for the lower chimney section.

NOTE: If you choose other chimney materials such as PEZ® or mocha beans, construction is done in the same fashion.

Sugar Work

1. Tape a piece of nonstick parchment to an inverted cookie sheet along the side edges only.

2. Slip the sugar work patterns for your particular building under the parchment.

3. Fill an icing bag with royal icing.

4. Pipe the designs according to the patterns with the house. Set aside to dry. (It is wise to make extras of each item as backups in case of breakage.)

5. When your sugar work decorations are completely dry (overnight is best) *carefully* remove them from the parchment and attach them in place with icing.

6. Pipe any decorative work on the house that you desire. This includes window and door outlines, signs, or lettering.

7. Pipe decorative beading over wall seams.

8. Finish with decorative work on eaves and ridgepole of roof using a star pastry tip.

SUGAR WORK FIGURES

1. For solid figures such as dogs, pipe icing heavily around outlines of designs and fill in area, building up frosting to create depth in muzzle area and front paws. Let dry overnight.

2. Remove from parchment. Repipe onto back for stability. Let dry and set in place with icing.

FLOOD WORK

Flood work is a technique of covering a surface with different colors of icing to result in a smooth finish.

1. Transfer the lined patterns to the cookies either freehand or by piercing holes in the patterns along the lines. Place the newly perforated pattern on the cookie and rub powdered sugar into the holes.

2. Decide what color each section will be and make the necessary colors of icing. Use throwaway parchment icing bags for this purpose as you will need quite a few.

3. Outline the area to be colored with the desired shade. Let set. To keep the same color, use the icing out of the bag and pipe enough to cover the area onto a saucer.

4. Dip a small paintbrush into water and stir the drop into the icing. Continue this process, one drop at a time, until the icing has the consistency of sour cream.

5. Using the paintbrush, start at one edge of the section to be colored and work your way in one direction to the opposite edge. Always work from the wet edge, or ridges will develop in the surface. The icing forms a crust very quickly, but it is still necessary to let it dry thoroughly overnight.

EVERGREEN TREE

Pipe green icing onto an inverted sugar cone with a #67 leaf tip, icing from bottom to top. Make one row around open edge in a wavelike motion, continuing up the cone to the top. Sprinkle green sugar crystals onto wet icing. Do not roll the trees in the sprinkles because the frosting will flatten. Set aside to dry.

NOTE: Leave the tip of the cone uniced so you have something to hold on to. Ice the tip last when the cone is in place to dry. Use small and large cones to produce the best effect.

GARLAND

Gather your green sugar sequins in a saucer. Pipe a scallop of icing under one window at a time and set green sequins one at a time into the icing with a pair of tweezers. When the first scallop is completed, move on to the second. Continue until you have enough garlands to suit your tastes. You may add red nonpareils for berries using tweezers.

WREATH

Pipe a half circle of icing onto the gingerbread wall. Do half the wreath at a time so the icing is wet and will hold the decorations. Set the green sugar sequins in the same fashion. Complete the circle. Add red nonpareils for berries with a pair of tweezers. To make the bow, use one red gumdrop and flatten it with your fingers. Dip it in sugar as needed to keep it from sticking. With a small pair of scissors, cut out a bow shape and apply it to the wreath with a dab of icing.

SNOWMAN

Use approximately 1/4 cup of icing and stir in powdered sugar until very stiff. Roll portions of icing into three balls of decreasing size. Set the largest one on the bottom, the middle-size one on top of that, and the smallest one on top. Insert a toothpick through all three snowballs for stability. Poke holes in the head for eyes, nose, and mouth. Use chocolate sprinkles as coal for the eyes. A marzipan carrot is used for the nose. Color a bit of marzipan red. Roll it into a snake, then flatten the ends and wrap it around the snowman's neck as a scarf. Clip the ends of the scarf to make fringe. The hat is made by cutting the top off a green gumdrop. Place this on the head and pipe a brim of green icing.

SHOVEL

Cut a piece of licorice gum in the shape desired. Curve the blade of the shovel slightly. Attach a 2" pretzel handle with icing. Let dry before positioning.

RAIL FENCE

Use long, thin pretzel sticks. The ones that come in snack-sized boxes are much longer than those in bags and should not be confused with pretzel rods that are used as logs. You need fence sections that are about 4" long. Lay three long pretzel sticks parallel to each other approximately 5/8" apart. Break off three pretzels to a length of 2 1/2". Pipe a dab of icing toward each end and center of each long pretzel stick. Make sure your parallel rows are even. Icing side up, apply fence posts, three per section. Repeat this as many times as necessary according to the specific house instructions. Let dry completely.

NOTE: For picket or iron fences, follow directions for sugar work.

LAMP POST

1. Using two very large yellow jelly candies (BRACH®'s makes Fruit Bunch® fruit-shaped jellies that work well), cut the thin layer of sugar from the flat side of each piece. Press the two sticky sides together.
2. Using a sharp knife, hollow out a hole in the base of the candies large enough to accommodate the diameter of a candy stick lamp post.
3. Pipe a bit of icing in the hole and insert the stick.
4. Cut off the top of the jelly candy so that it is flat and pipe four lines from top to bottom, equally spaced around the light.
5. Pipe a cap on the lamp and a ring of icing around the light base where the candy stick post enters the jelly candy. Set aside to dry by standing the pole in a glass or rice-filled cup.

STONE WALL

1. Build your candy pebble stone wall on your board first before you add any snow or grass. Decide where your stone wall should be and pipe a thick line of icing and set first row of stones into it.
2. Begin the second row making certain there is some icing between every stone. Work your way around the wall to a height of about three stones. Work slowly so the icing has a chance to set between each layer.

TREE STUMP

1. Cut a length four sections long from a large Tootsie Roll®, leaving the sections connected. Heat in a microwave oven or warm spot until pliable.

2. Roll into a log shape, short and squat. With a knife, make uneven 1/4" deep cuts in base and separate these into roots by pulling and shaping.

3. Make certain the top is flat and cut a small slit in top where the axe will be positioned. Score lines in the sides to simulate bark.

4. To create the axe, using one purple Necco® candy wafer, break off opposite sides with your thumbnail. Break off a 2" piece of a pretzel stick and attach to axehead with a dab of frosting. Let dry.

WALKWAY

Slate

On brown paper that covers the board, draw your walkway lines using pencil or waterproof marker. Pipe approximately 2" of icing between the lines, completely covering the area. Using broken Necco® candy wafers in black, brown, and purple, set into the icing in a jigsaw fashion. Continue in this manner until your walkway is complete.

Stepping stone

Cut stepping stone shapes out of licorice gum. When you are ready to cover your board with grass or snow, ice the section of board larger than where your stepping stone walkway will be. If you are using grass, the icing will be green. Set the stones in place and immediately cover the wet icing with grass. If it is a winter scene, continue frosting the board in white.

Shoveled

Frost the board to a depth of about 1/4". To "shovel" the walk, push the icing to each side and make small mounds. Sprinkle sanding sugar over snow, leaving walkway clear. Pepper that with chocolate sprinkles.

GRASS

To tint the coconut green for grass, place one package of shredded coconut in a bowl with a plastic lid. Mix 20 drops of liquid food coloring into the bowl and cover with lid. Shake vigorously until color is evenly dispersed.

DIRT

Cover the area with brown icing and lightly sprinkle with unsweetened cocoa powder.

Gingerbread Houses

Victorian Farmhouse

THE DOG WAITS on the porch to greet holiday guests. The lights inside promise a cozy welcome to all who visit.

MATERIALS

plywood board 16 x 16 x 1/2"
brown paper
masking tape
1 1/2 batches dough
2 batches royal icing
30 packages (or 150 sticks) of licorice gum (Black Jack®)
chocolate caramels
Necco® candy wafers (black, brown, and purple)
3 candy sticks or canes
sanding sugar
pretzel sticks
colored nonpareils
sugar sequins (green)
sugar cones (small and large)
green sugar crystals
paste food coloring (green)
gumdrops (red)
lace (optional)
votive candle with candle holder (optional)

INSTRUCTIONS

1. Cover plywood board according to general instructions (p. 13) and prepare dough according to recipe (p. 12).

2. Cut out and bake the following pieces:
VICTORIAN FARMHOUSE
gable left side wall—1
gable front—1
gable right side wall—1
front wall—1
right side wall—1
back wall—1
gable roof left—1
gable roof right—1
main roof front—1
main roof back—1
porch floor—1
porch roof —1
bottom step—1
middle step—1
top step—1
porch front support—1
porch side support—1

NOTE: If you would like lace curtains in the windows, attach them with a dab of icing before putting the roof in place. If you would like a Christmas tree in the window, decorate and put it in place with icing before roofing the house.

3. Assemble house as per general instructions (p. 13) on board.

4. Using icing, attach porch supports using the same method as for the walls. Let dry several minutes.

5. Pipe icing onto the top edge of the supports and on the porch floor where it will join the walls of the house.

6. Put porch floor in place. Let dry at least 1 hour.

7. With a sharp serrated knife, saw the hooked ends off three candy canes (or use peppermint sticks if they are about 3 1/2" long). It is important that all canes are the same length.

8. Pipe a bit of icing on each end of all three candy sticks. Set them on a baking rack temporarily. Pipe icing on the porch roof edges that will join the walls of the house. Using one candy stick for height, apply the porch roof to the house, resting the porch roof on the end of the candy stick. Place the second candy stick carefully under the edge of the roof. Repeat with the third candy stick. (At this point it may help to have an extra hand to hold a candy stick in place.) Add extra

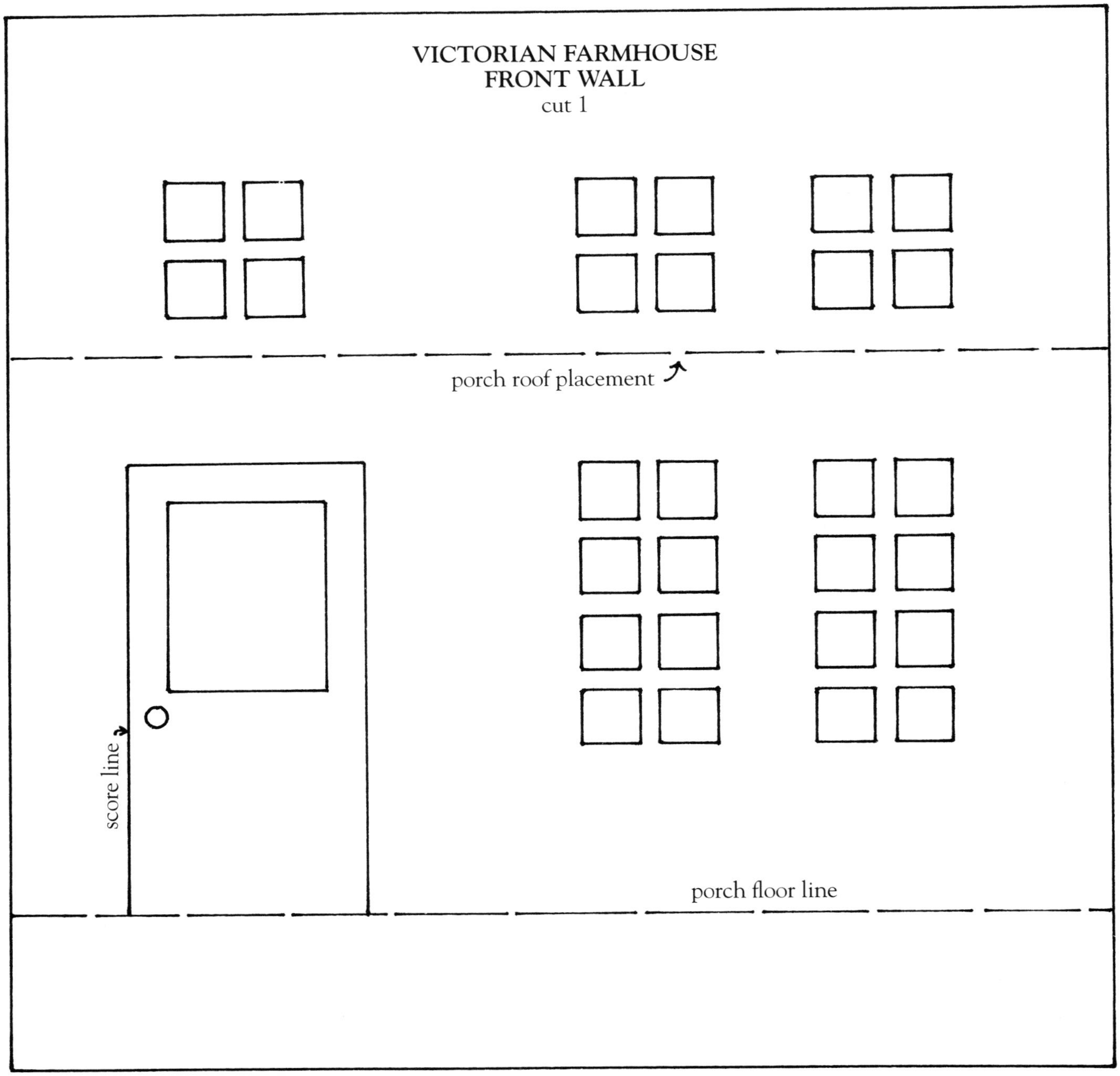

**VICTORIAN FARMHOUSE
FRONT WALL
cut 1**

porch roof placement

porch floor line

score line

**VICTORIAN FARMHOUSE
PORCH FRONT SUPPORT
cut 1**

**FRONT PORCH DOG
(SUGAR WORK)**

**VICTORIAN
FARMHOUSE
PORCH SIDE
SUPPORT**
cut 1

**VICTORIAN
FARMHOUSE
TOP STEP**
cut 1

**VICTORIAN
FARMHOUSE
MIDDLE STEP**
cut 1

**VICTORIAN FARMHOUSE
BOTTOM STEP**
cut 1

icing to the seam where the porch roof joins the house if necessary. Hold this in place for a few minutes until the icing sets.

9. Pipe icing to the bottom side of the first stair section and place on the board against the porch support in front of the door. Add the second stair in the same manner on top of the first stair. Complete with the third stair.

10. To shingle the roof, you will need about thirty packages (150 sticks) of licorice gum, each piece cut in thirds. Shingle the roof (p. 16) and to complete, pipe a decorative bead of icing across the ridgepole using a star pastry tip.

11. Make the chimney using light and/or dark caramels (p. 16).

12. Pipe the fancywork for the roof peak and porch railings. Let dry. Attach to house with icing.

13. Make a dog (p. 18). Let dry.

14. Make a snowman (p. 19). Let dry.

15. Make a shovel (p. 20). Let dry.

16. Make trees (p. 19). All the sugar work may be made a day in advance so they will be completely dry.

17. Make the foundation with broken Necco® candy wafers.

18. Apply garlands and wreath (p. 19) to the house using the photograph as a guide.

19. Spread 1/4″ of icing on the board. To "shovel" a walkway, push the icing off to each side to create mounds of snow. Sprinkle the walkway with crushed chocolate sprinkles.

20. Carefully set all accessories in place with icing. Set spearmint leaf shrubs in place.

21. Pipe decorative beading on all seams and any unfinished edges of the house and raw edges, using small squirts of royal icing using a star or round pastry tip.

22. Place a votive candle (contained in a candle holder) in the house if desired.

NOTE: It is possible to put footprints in the snow after the walkway is laid but before the icing has dried completely. Use a small piece of crumpled foil and make footprints through the snow, across the walkway, and up the porch steps.

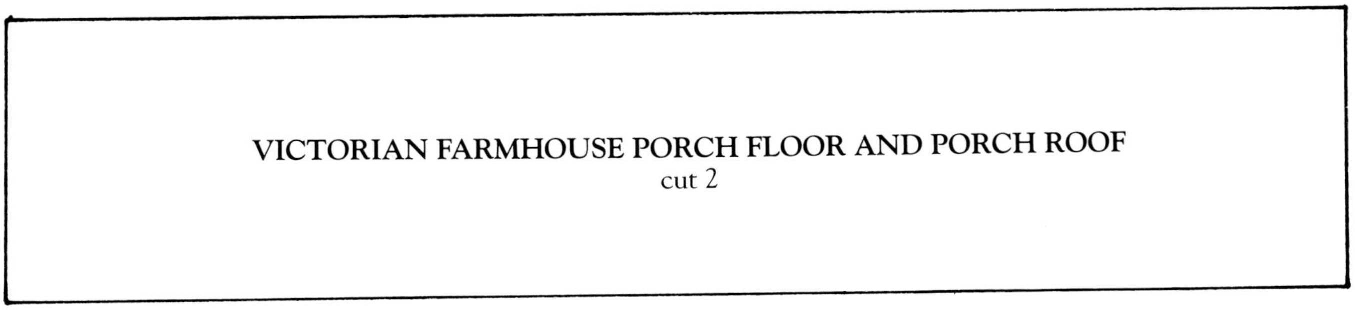

VICTORIAN FARMHOUSE PORCH FLOOR AND PORCH ROOF
cut 2

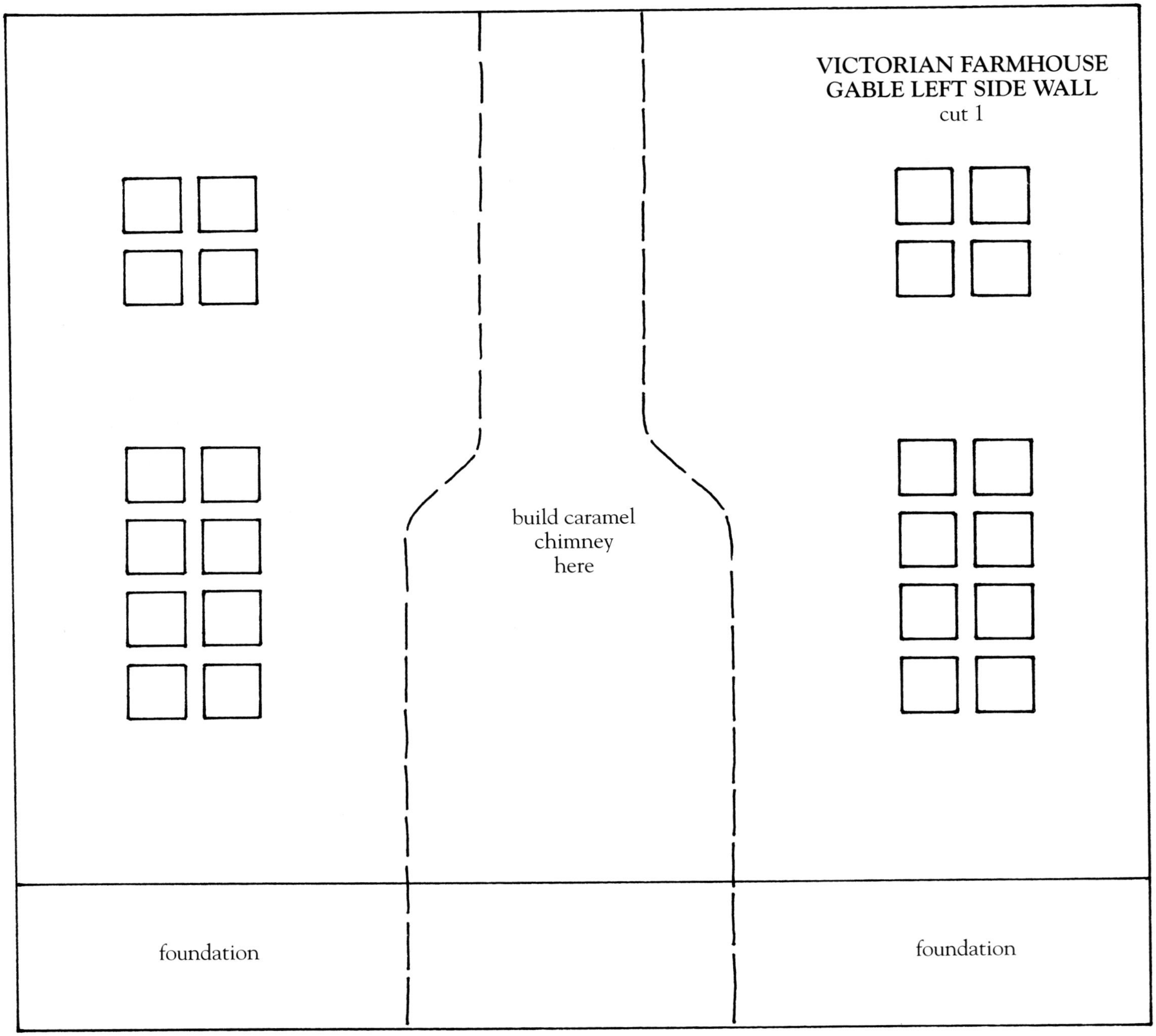

**VICTORIAN FARMHOUSE
GABLE LEFT SIDE WALL**
cut 1

build caramel
chimney
here

foundation

foundation

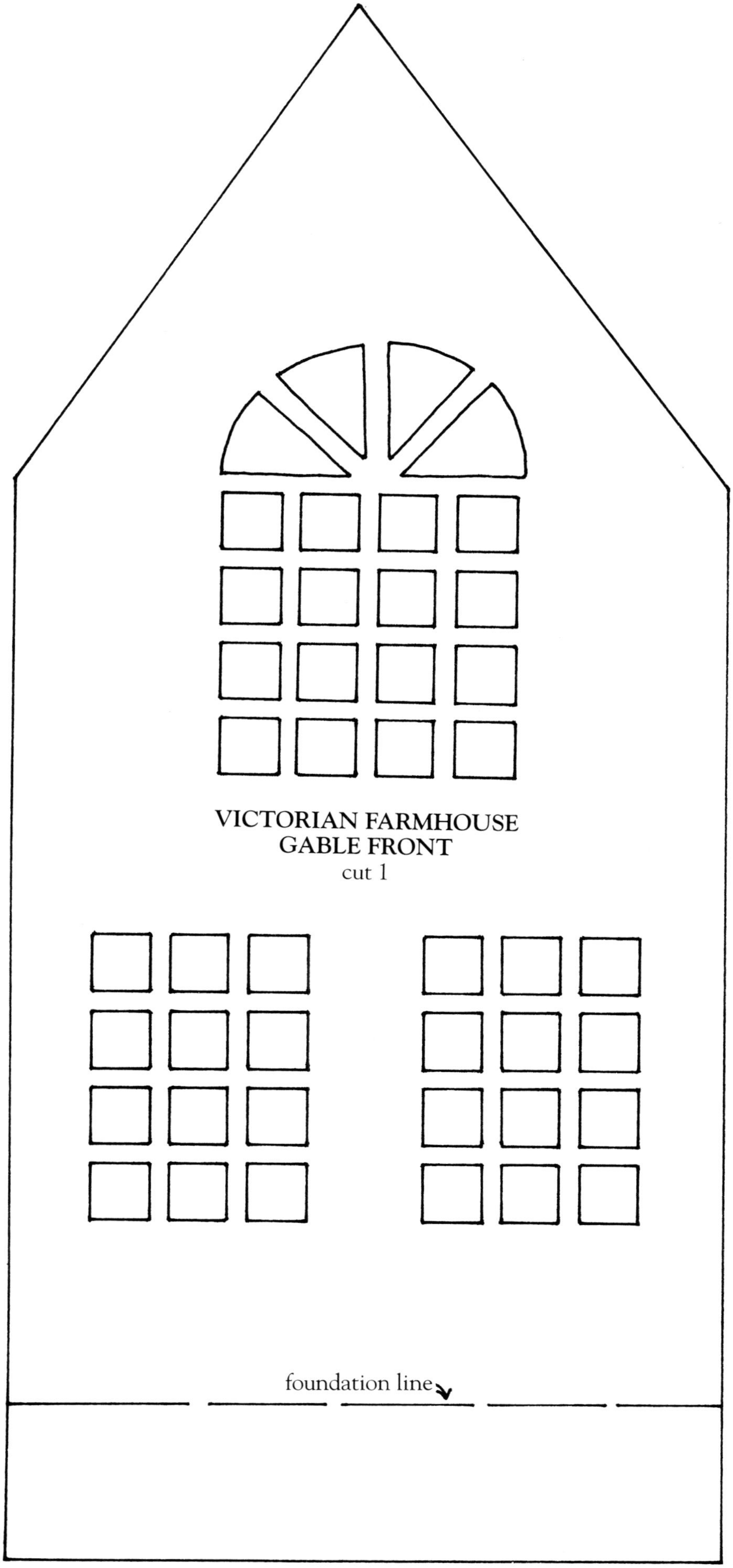

**VICTORIAN FARMHOUSE
GABLE FRONT**
cut 1

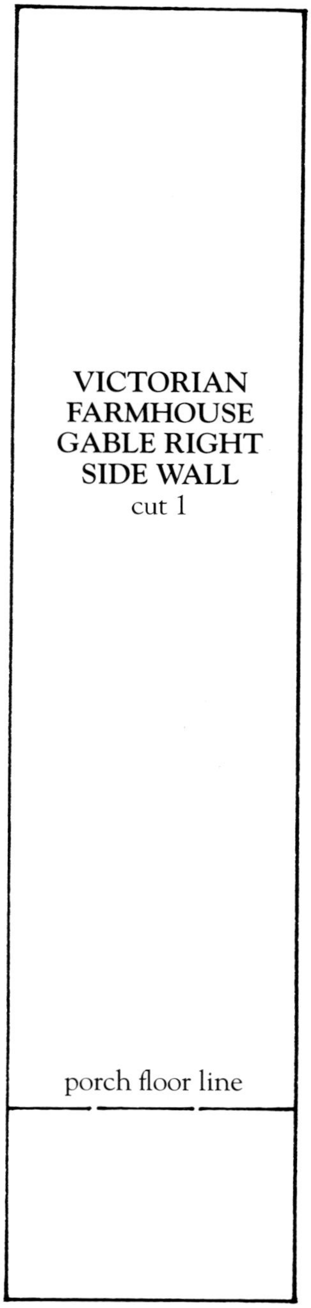

**VICTORIAN
FARMHOUSE
GABLE RIGHT
SIDE WALL**
cut 1

foundation line

porch floor line

**GABLE PEAK FANCY
(SUGAR WORK)**

VICTORIAN FARMHOUSE BACK WALL

Note: Tape to other half of back
pattern piece along dotted
line, then cut 1.

tape to other half of back here

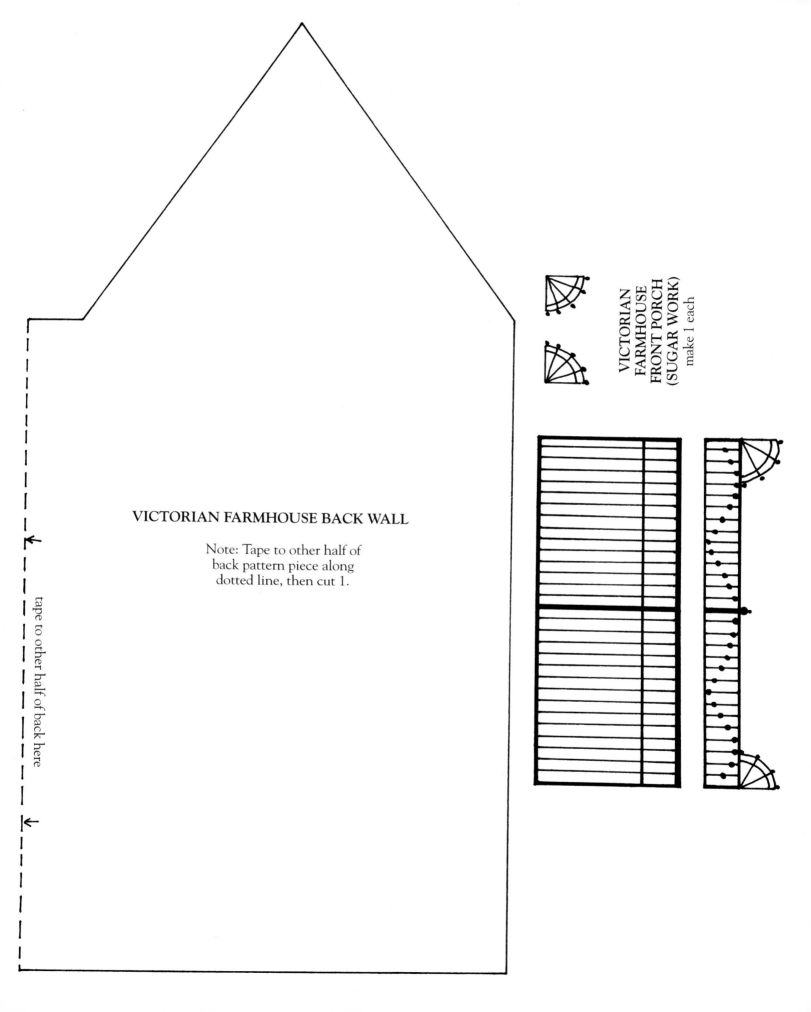

VICTORIAN FARMHOUSE BACK WALL

Note: Tape to other half of
back pattern piece along
dotted line, then cut 1.

tape to other half of back here

VICTORIAN
FARMHOUSE
FRONT PORCH
(SUGAR WORK)
make 1 each

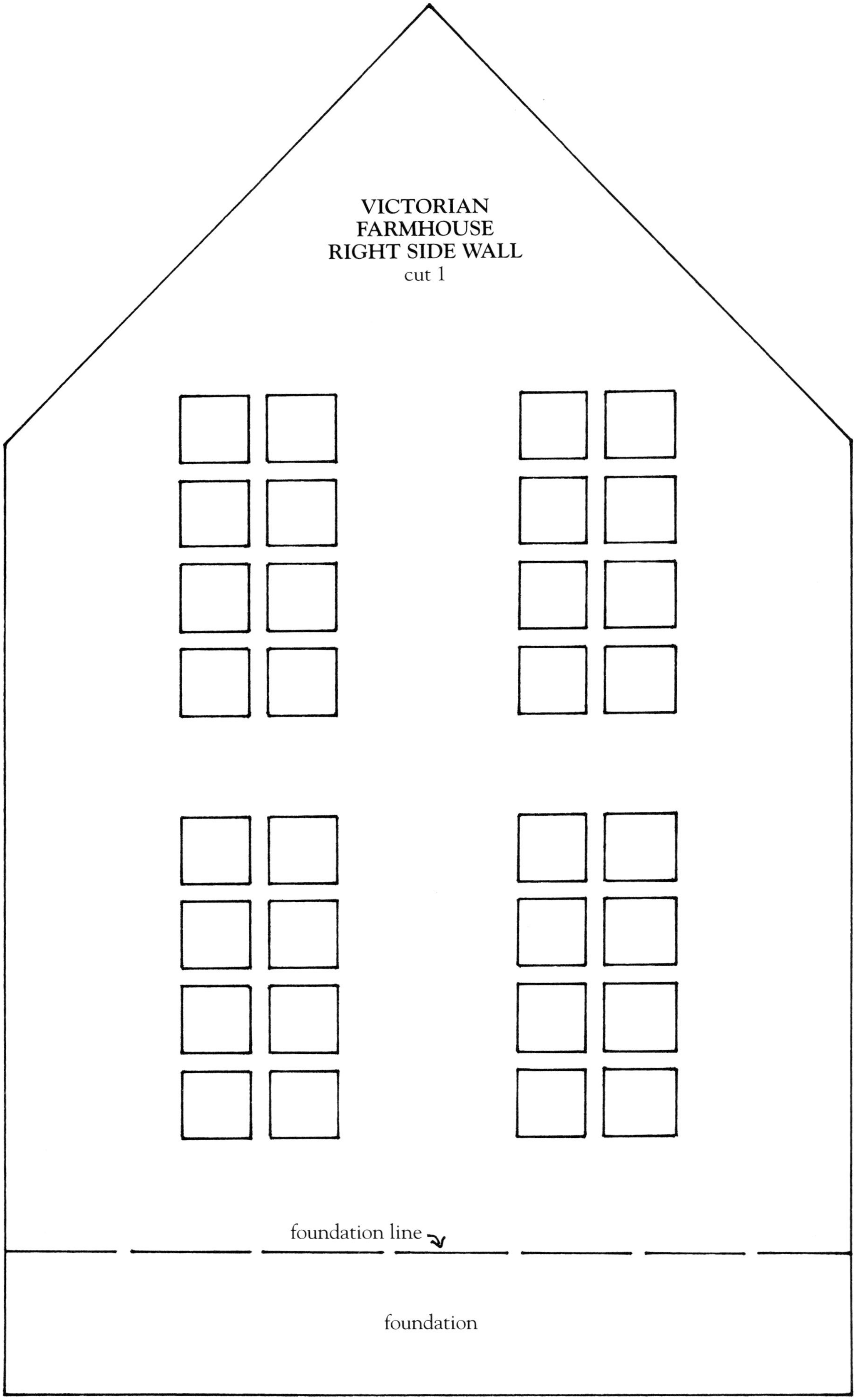

**VICTORIAN
FARMHOUSE
RIGHT SIDE WALL**
cut 1

foundation line ↴

foundation

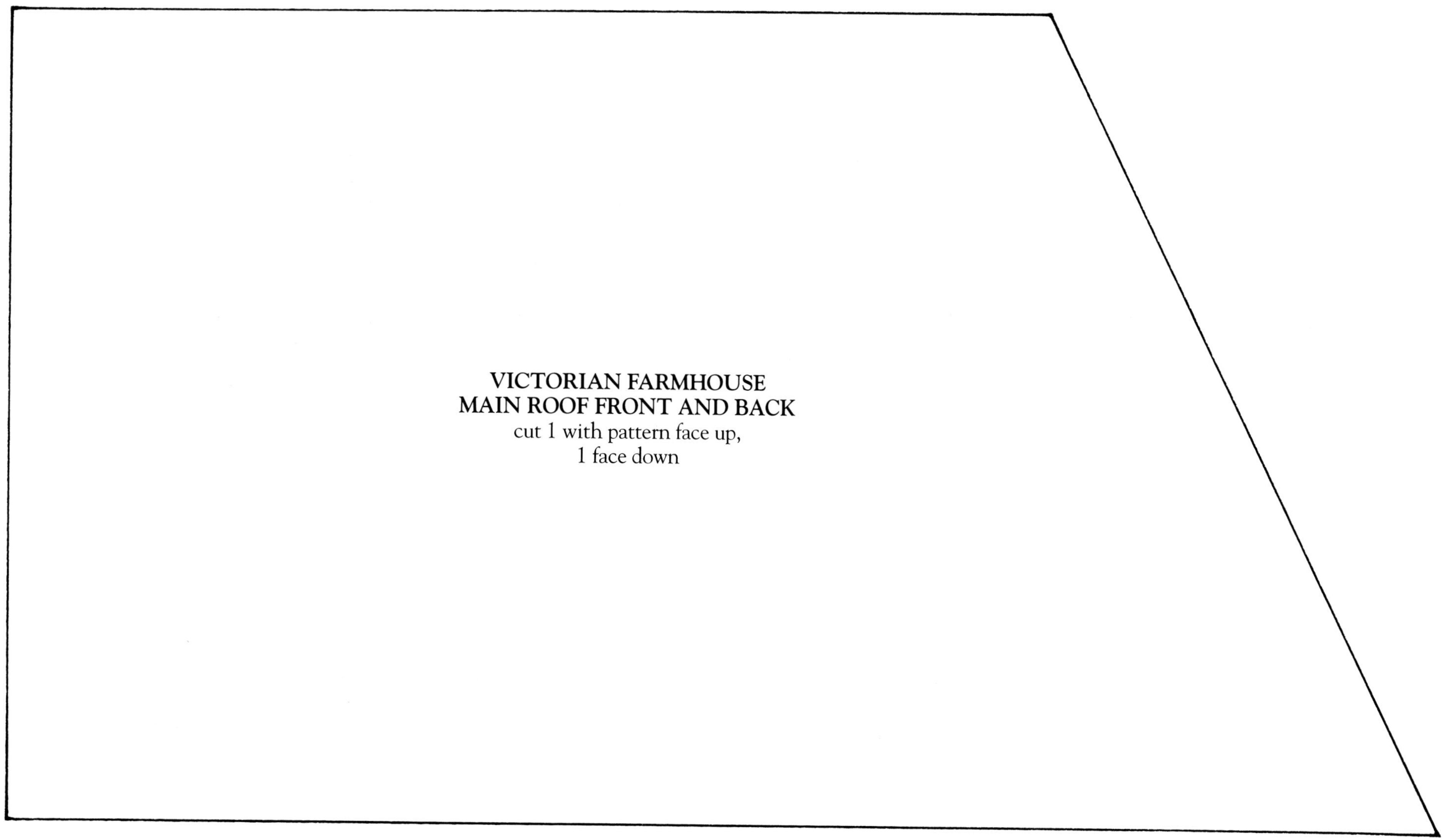

VICTORIAN FARMHOUSE
MAIN ROOF FRONT AND BACK
cut 1 with pattern face up,
1 face down

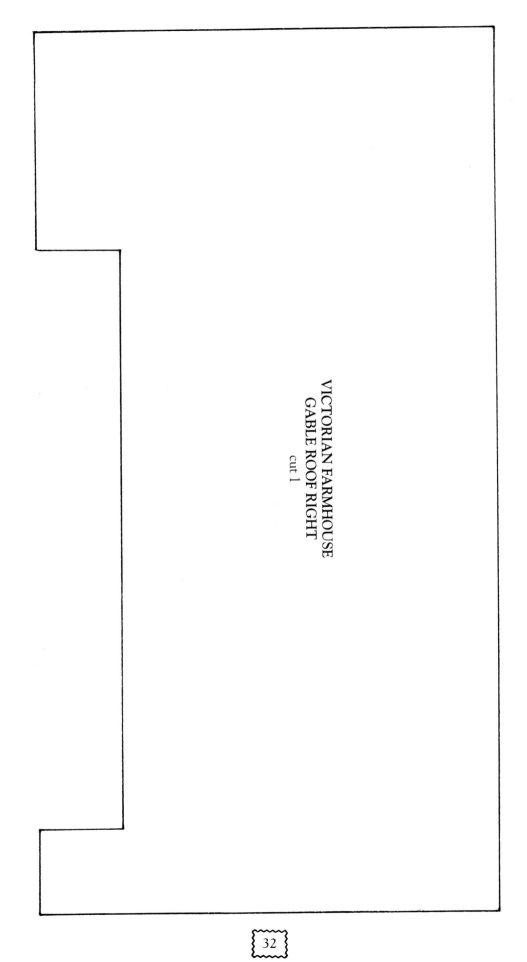

VICTORIAN FARMHOUSE
GABLE ROOF RIGHT

cut 1

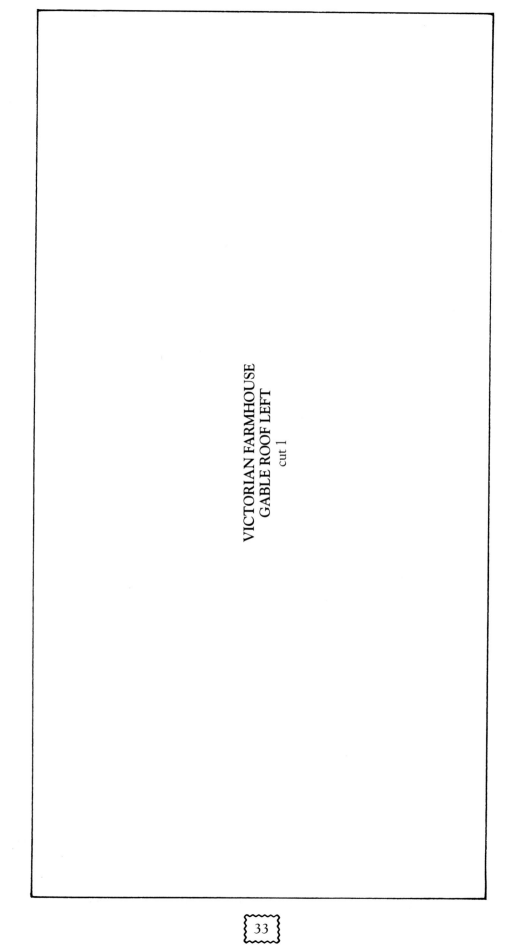

VICTORIAN FARMHOUSE
GABLE ROOF LEFT
cut 1

Barn

WHO EVER SAID that gingerbread houses could only represent winter scenes? The animals in this barnyard, with its flourishing vegetable garden, think of winter only as a fond memory as they bask in the sun and try to nibble the grass on the other side of the fence.

MATERIALS

plywood board 22 x 22 x 1/2"
brown paper
masking tape
cardboard tube 2 1/2" in diameter (wrapping paper tube will work)
1 batch dough
3 batches royal icing
powdered food coloring (red or burgundy and blue)
paste food color
liquid food color (green)
1 box Keebler® Sun Toasted Wheats crackers
2 7-ounce packages shredded coconut
cocoa powder
pretzel sticks (long and thin)
licorice gum (Black Jack®)
small amount of marzipan
small piece of muslin or fiddler's cloth
2 tablespoons uncooked rice
sugar sequins (yellow)
small, stiff-bristle paintbrush

INSTRUCTIONS

1. Cover plywood board according to general instructions (p. 13) and prepare dough according to recipe (p. 12).
2. Cut and bake the following pieces:
BARN
front—1
back—1
side wall—2
upper and lower barn door—4
loft door—2
upper roof—2
lower roof—2
hayloft—1

**BARN
SILO WALL
cut 8**

**BARN CAP
(UNDER SILO ROOF)
cut 1**

**BARN DOORS
UPPER AND LOWER**
cut 4

**BARN
LOFT DOORS**
cut 2

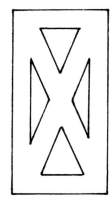

hayloft support—3
silo wall—8
cap (under silo roof)—1
silo roof—bake 1
animals as desired

NOTE: Cut barn and loft doors, upper and lower, in front piece only. Silo roof can be formed and baked over one cup of an inverted muffin tin.

3. To make the silo roof, roll out the gingerbread dough and cut out a circular piece slightly larger than required. Spray the bottom of one cup of a muffin tin with a non-stick cooking spray. Drape dough and gently form it over the mold, making sure there are no cracks. Trim off extra with a sharp knife, taking care to cut as closely and evenly to the base as possible. Pierce the top of the gingerbread (as you would for pie crust to avoid air bubbles) and bake.

4. When all the sections are baked and cooled, you are ready to color the front, back, and side walls red. Rub powdered food color onto baked gingerbread with a firm paintbrush, creating a weathered look.

5. On the back side of the front, just under the loft window, attach hayloft piece and supports. Let dry.

6. Assemble the barn as per general directions (p. 13).

7. For the silo, cut a piece of 2 1/2" diameter cardboard tubing 8 1/2" in length. Using a #4 pastry tip, pipe icing along silo wall sections. Attach these to cardboard tube lengthwise. Let dry.

8. Stand the silo on the left front corner of the barn where the notch is cut out of the roof. Using icing, attach the cap to the top of the silo. Cut licorice gum in thirds and apply to silo in rows, trimming gum where needed to create a cinder block effect.

9. Rub dry blue powdered food coloring into the silo roof and attach to silo with icing.

10. Shingle the barn roof with small, hexagonal crackers (Keebler® Sun Toasted Wheats).

11. Outline the windows with a #2 pastry tip and white icing. Outline the doors and cross bucks. Using a star pastry tip, run a line of small beads along the ridgepole of roof and eaves.

12. Using the flood work technique (p. 18), pipe the chickens and decorate the animal cookies (p. 18) or use your own imagination.

13. Make the rail fence (p. 20). Let dry completely.

14. Make the shovel (p. 20).

15. Make the vegetables (pumpkins, carrot tops, red cabbage) by coloring then shaping small amounts of marzipan into vegetables desired. A small piece of parsley can top a carrot as with other greenery.

16. Make grass using tinted coconut (p. 21).

17. Make brown icing by adding cocoa or brown food coloring to icing. Make green icing in the same manner.

18. On your board, designate your fence line. Spread brown icing inside the fence line and sprinkle lightly with powdered cocoa. To create your garden, do the same. Cover all other exposed areas with green icing and top with green coconut.

19. Using brown icing, pipe dabs onto bottom of each fence post and place around the fence line. Plant your marzipan vegetables in garden. Using yellow sugar sequins, dot your lawn with buttercups.

20. Tint a small amount of coconut a golden yellow color. Place in hayloft with icing and hang some strands out the loft door. Nest the chicken on the hay.

21. Position your decorated animals around the barnyard.

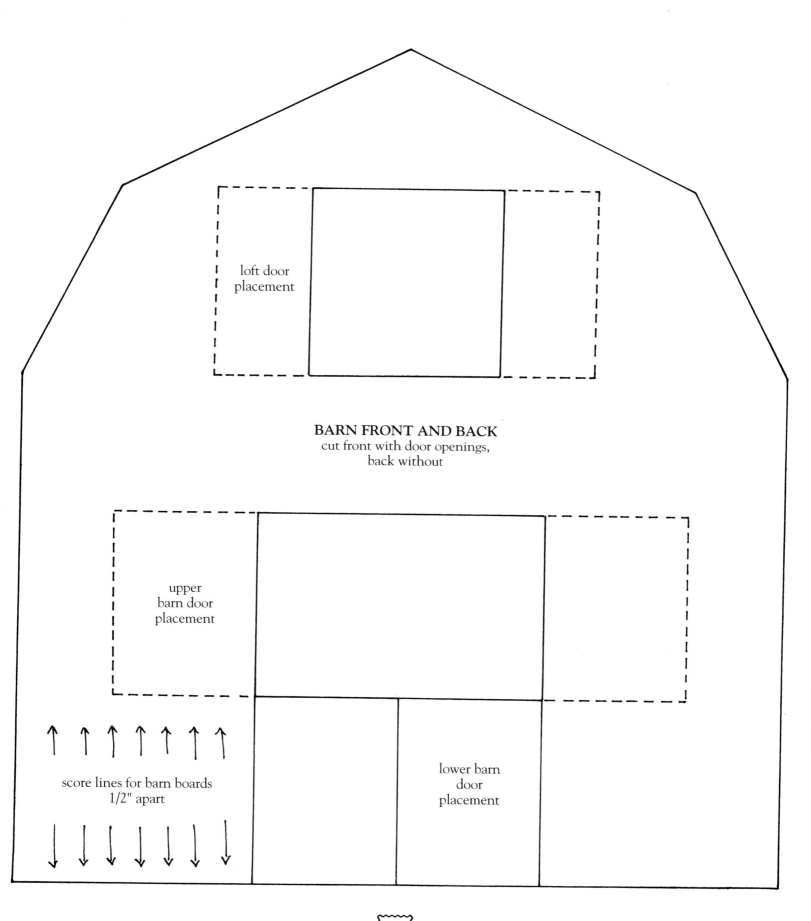

loft door
placement

BARN FRONT AND BACK
cut front with door openings,
back without

upper
barn door
placement

lower barn
door
placement

score lines for barn boards
1/2" apart

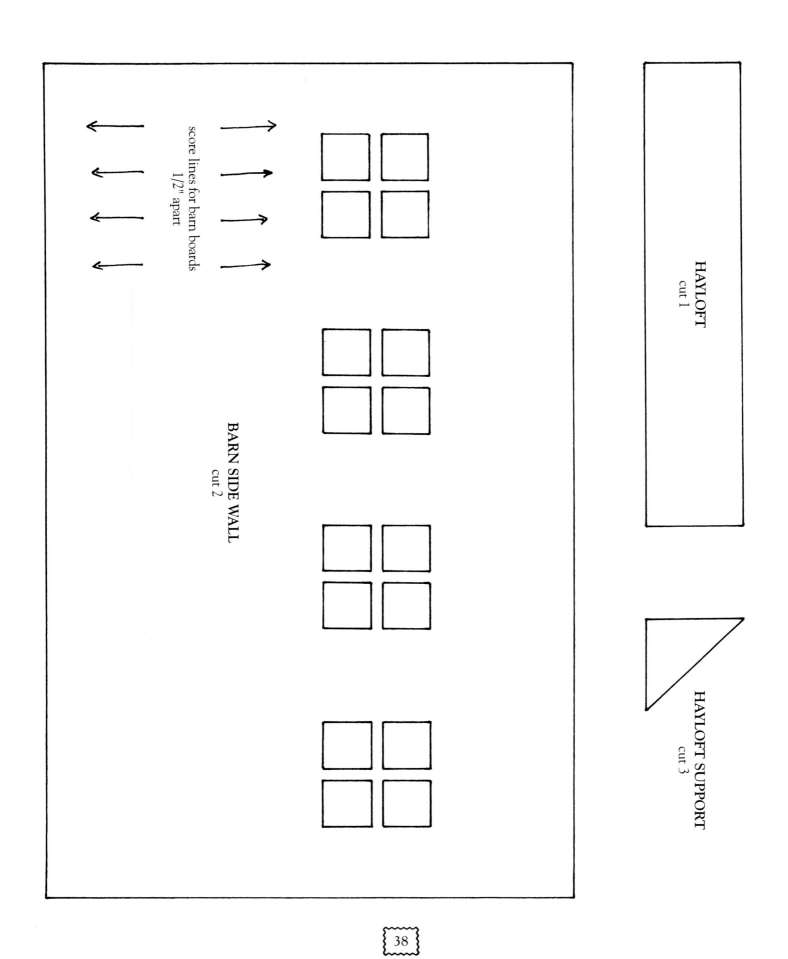

HAYLOFT
cut 1

HAYLOFT SUPPORT
cut 3

BARN SIDE WALL
cut 2

score lines for barn boards
1/2" apart

ANIMALS
(FLOODWORK ON GINGERBREAD)

HAYLOFT CHICKEN
(SUGAR WORK)

BARNYARD CHICKENS
(SUGAR WORK)

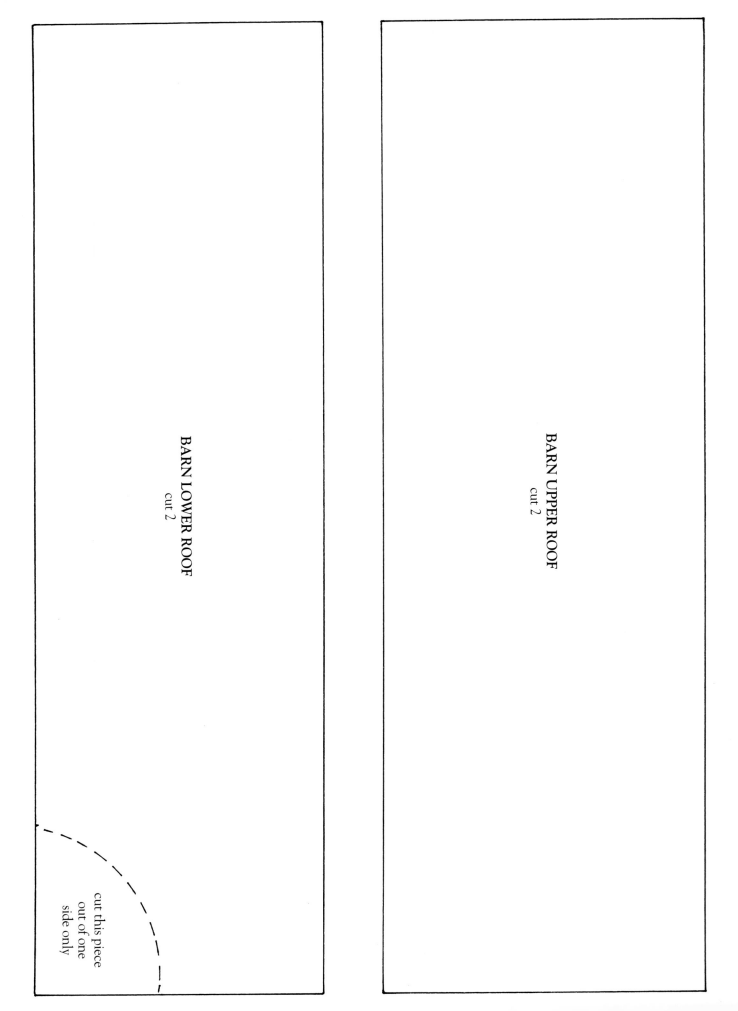

BARN LOWER ROOF
cut 2

cut this piece
out of one
side only

BARN UPPER ROOF
cut 2

SKI CHALET

IT COULD BE in the Rocky Mountains, the Green Mountains, Canada, or just moments away from your own home; the ski chalet offers a winter vacation treat for all.

MATERIALS

plywood board 15 x 15 x 1/2″
brown paper
masking tape
1 batch dough
2 batches royal icing
30 packages (150 sticks) of cinnamon gum (Big Red®)
small amount of marzipan
chocolate sprinkles
gumdrops (green)
colored sprinkles
sugar cones (small and large)
green sugar crystals
white sugar crystals (sanding sugar)
paste food colors
1 stick licorice gum (Black Jack®)
1 pretzel stick

INSTRUCTIONS

1. Cover plywood board according to general instructions (p. 13) and prepare dough according to recipe (p. 12).
2. Cut out and bake the following pieces:
SKI CHALET
front—1
back—1
side wall—2
roof—2

NOTE: Score the door outline into the dough and cut window openings on the front piece only before baking. If you want curtains on the windows, they must be attached before the roof is put in place. Strips of lace can be glued in with icing.

3. Assemble as per general instructions (p. 13).
4. Do not skimp with icing when attaching the roof as these pieces are heavy and require extra help to stay in place. The roof is shingled with cinnamon gum and requires thirty packs. Cut each piece into three equal sections and continue as per the instructions (p. 15), covering the roof completely.
5. Using candy sticks or the straight part of a candy cane, set these along ridgepole of roof with icing.
6. Make one large and two small trees (p. 19).
7. Pipe sugar work (p. 19). Let dry completely.
8. Place the sugar work balcony floor on a piece of wax paper. Assemble balcony. Attach the balcony front to the balcony floor at a 90° angle. Attach the balcony sides to the floor and the front. Let dry. Proceed with the window boxes in the same manner.
9. Attach dove wing to its body with a dab of icing. Attach doves over the door. Once the balcony and window boxes are dry, attach them to the chalet with a line of piped icing along the connecting edges. Carefully hold it in place until set.
10. Make a snowman (p. 19).
11. Make a snow or spade shovel (p. 20).
12. Using royal icing and an icing spatula, spread frosting evenly over the "ground" to a 1/4" depth. We recommend not to cover the sides of the board; you can wrap a ribbon around it later. Sprinkle with sanding or coarse sugar crystals. Place ice cream cone trees in position. Make a path using chocolate sprinkles. Set snowman and shovel in place with icing.

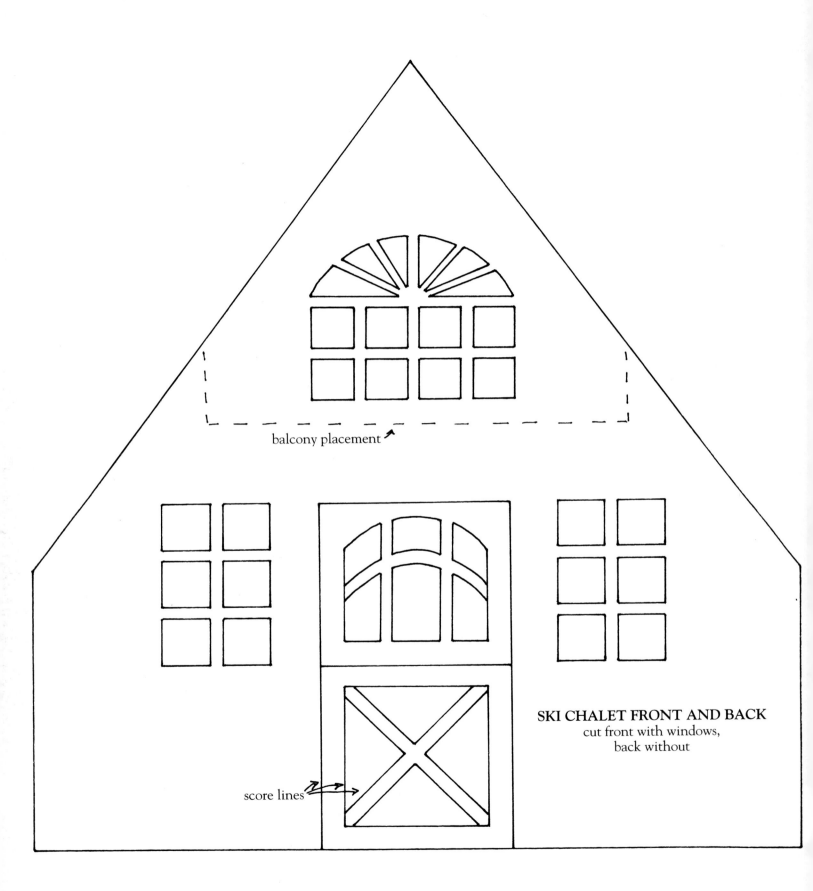

balcony placement ↗

SKI CHALET FRONT AND BACK
cut front with windows,
back without

score lines →→

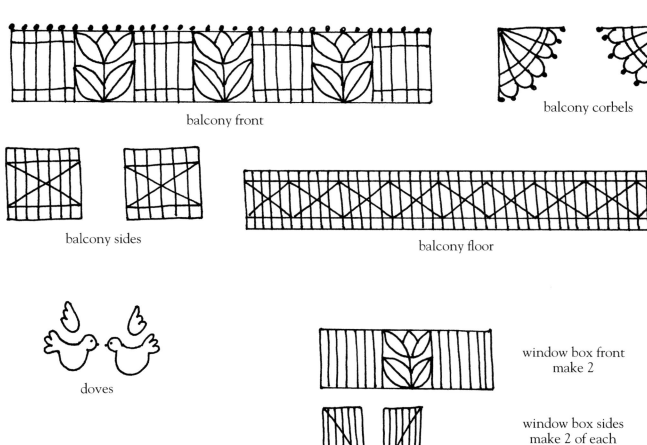

balcony front

balcony corbels

balcony sides

balcony floor

doves

**SKI CHALET
(SUGAR WORK)**

window box front
make 2

window box sides
make 2 of each

window box bottom
make 2

SKI CHALET SIDE WALL
cut 2

tape to other half here

SKI CHALET ROOF

Note: Make 2 roof sections: tape 2
halves of this pattern piece together
to make 1 roof pattern.
Then cut 2 from gingerbread.

Woodsman's Cabin

THE HOLIDAY SEASON comes to all corners of the country, even a remote cabin nestled in the woods. Those inside curl up in front of a crackling fire with a cup of hot cocoa. A pile of wood stacked just outside the door ensures that the fire never ceases to warm the home.

MATERIALS

plywood board 15 x 15 x 1/2"
brown paper
masking tape
1 batch dough
1 1/2 batches royal icing
2 6-ounce cans pecan halves
chocolate caramels
lace
sugar sequins (green)
colored nonpareils
gumdrops (red)
pretzel rods
pretzel sticks
Necco® candy wafers (purple)
1 Tootsie Roll® (large)
chocolate sprinkles
sugar cones (small and large)
green sugar crystals
1 cotton ball
votive candle in a candle holder (optional)

INSTRUCTIONS

1. Cover plywood board according to general instructions (p. 13) and prepare dough according to recipe (p. 12).
2. Cut out and bake the following pieces:
WOODSMAN'S CABIN
front—1
back—1
side wall—2
roof—2

3. Assemble the cabin as per general instructions (p. 13).

NOTE: If you want curtains on the windows, they must be attached before the roof is put in place. Strips of lace can be glued in with icing.

4. Make trees (p. 19).
5. Make a rail fence (p. 20).
6. Make a tree stump (p. 21).
7. Make an axe (p. 21).
8. Using a serrated knife, saw large pretzel rods into 12 1 1/4" lengths. These will be your firewood. Set aside.
9. Build the chimney as per the instructions (p. 16) using chocolate caramels with nuts.
10. Using pecan halves, shingle roof according to directions (p. 16). Cover the entire roof front and back.
11. Make wreaths and garlands (p. 19).
12. To make icicles, use a #2 pastry tip and start at the eaves. Begin by squeezing the icing bag, but as you bring the bag gently downward, release the pressure. This will pull the icing to a point so that it resembles an icicle. Continue this process across the entire length of the eaves front and back.
13. Ice the board with a knife or spatula to a 1/4" depth. Pepper the walkway with chocolate sprinkles. Set each tree in place. Gently press the tree stump into the right front corner of the yard leaving room for the fence. Pushing only on the axe head, place the axe into the tree stump. Cross-stack the firewood in rows of three in front of the house, using icing to hold the sections together. Attach the fence by putting a dab of icing on each fence post and sticking it into the wet icing already on the board. Begin with the two sections in front of the house and work your way around to the sides.

NOTE: Flour sacks are available at miniature stores or you may make your own using small amounts of muslin stitched around the sides and filled with dry rice.

WOODSMAN'S CABIN
FRONT AND BACK WALLS
cut front with windows and door,
back without

score in lines for door

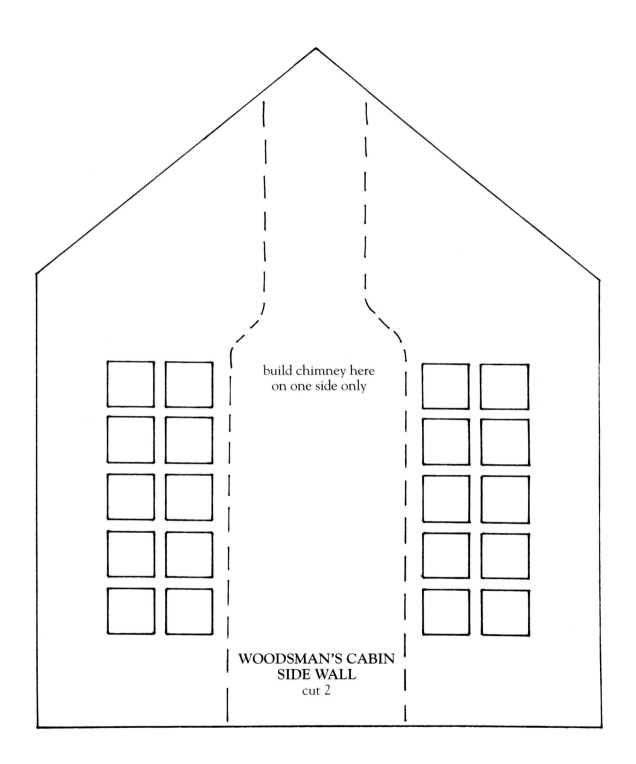

build chimney here
on one side only

**WOODSMAN'S CABIN
SIDE WALL**
cut 2

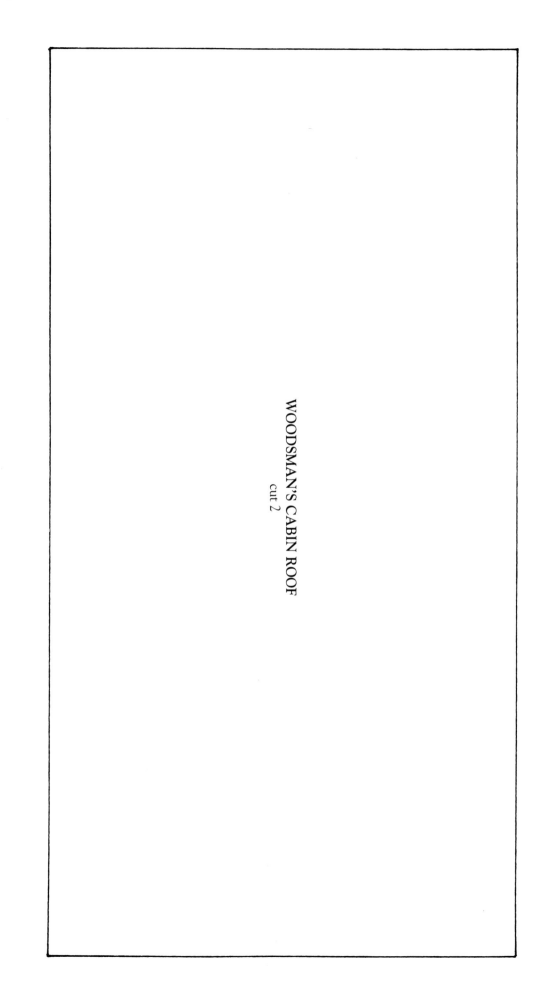

WOODSMAN'S CABIN ROOF

cut 2

SWEET SHOP

WHAT WOULD A village be without a sweet shop? Tasty treasures of sugar and spice, confections to tempt and to delight await inside.

MATERIALS

plywood board 15 x 15 x 1/2"
brown paper
masking tape
drill and drill bit
1 batch dough
1 1/2 batches royal icing
paste food colors
liquid food color (green)
Necco® candy wafers (rainbow colors and black,
brown, and purple)
1 7-ounce package shredded coconut
green sugar crystals
sugar cones (small and large)
3 candy sticks
small pretzel twists
spearmint leaves jelly candies
colorful candies for window displays
2 large yellow jelly candies (BRACH®'s Fruit Bunch®)
sugar sequins (red and green)
lace for curtains

INSTRUCTIONS

1. Cover plywood board according to general instructions (p. 13) and prepare dough according to recipe (p. 12).
2. Cut and bake the following pieces:
SWEET SHOP
front—1
back—1 (front with windows, back without)
side wall—2
roof—2

3. Make 1 1/2 batches royal icing.
4. Using a #2 writing pastry tip, pipe the peak fancy. Set aside to dry. Color 2 tablespoons of icing with red food coloring and 2 tablespoons with enough black to make a dark gray color. Pipe the dog in white icing and set aside to dry. Pipe the bicycle spokes in gray icing with a very tiny opening in the parchment bag. Next pipe the bicycle rims around the spokes. Using white icing, make whitewalls around the rims. Cut off the tip of the gray icing bag so that it is of a slightly larger diameter, then pipe the tires in gray icing. Using red icing, pipe the frame of the bicycle. Use dark gray icing for the seat and handlebars. Let dry. When the bike is dry, turn it over and repipe icing onto the back so it will be strong. Repipe the back of the dog with white. After the second application is dry, turn the dog over and add its features, eyes, nose, and spots, with black icing. Use red icing to create a bandanna. Let dry.

NOTE: These items may be made a day ahead so they are ready to use.

5. Assemble the shop as per general instructions (p. 13).
6. Shingle the roof with the material of your choice (p. 16). For the shop in the photograph, we used Necco® candy wafers in rainbow colors.
7. Cut two candy sticks on angles at the same height and that correspond with the angle on the roof. Attach these to the front two corners of the building with icing.
8. Using a #1 writing pastry tip, draw lines around the windows and other decorations you would like on the face of the building.
9. Carefully drill a hole in the board for the lamp post with a drill bit the same diameter as the candy stick.
10. Make a lamp post (p. 20).
11. Make one large tree and one small tree (p. 19).
12. Draw your walkway onto the brown paper covering your board. Pave the walkway with appropriate masonry (p. 21).
13. If you would like a summer scene, frost the board with green icing and cover with one batch of coconut grass (p. 21). For a winter scene, frost the board with white icing.
14. Use small snack-size pretzels lined up along each side of the walkway for a fence.
15. Set the trees in place.
16. Set the lamp post in place.
17. Carefully remove the peak fancy from the parchment. Ice the edges and attach to front roof eaves and hold gently until set.
18. Attach the dog with a bit of icing to the area in front of the door.
19. Carefully lean the bicycle up against the fence.

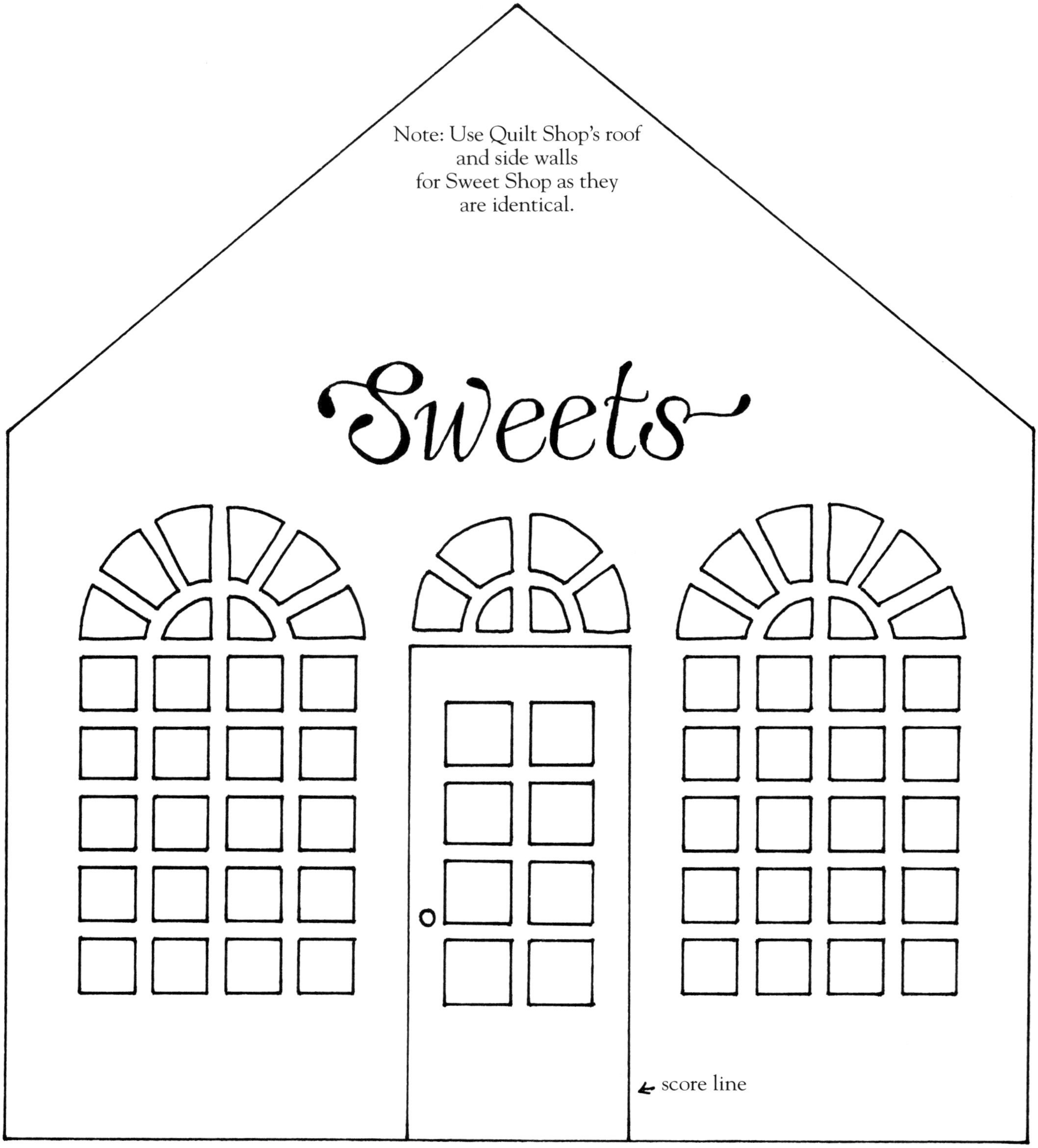

Note: Use Quilt Shop's roof
and side walls
for Sweet Shop as they
are identical.

Sweets

← score line

SWEET SHOP FRONT AND BACK
cut front with windows, back without

**SWEET SHOP PEAK FANCY
(SUGAR WORK)**

**SWEET SHOP DOG
(SUGAR WORK)**

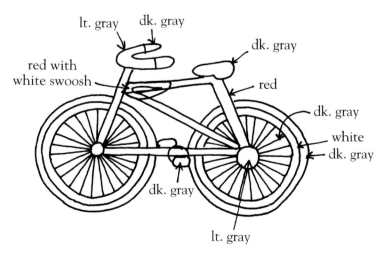

**BICYCLE
(SUGAR WORK)**

Note: Pipe in order of what is farthest from
the eye first, i.e., spokes, tires, frame, etc.
Let dry thoroughly (overnight) then *carefully*
turn over and repipe all except spokes.

COUNTRY STORE

"IF WE DON'T have it, you don't need it." The country store provides everything, including the freshest vegetables and the warmest of conversations with the storekeeper and his cat.

MATERIALS

plywood board 15 x 15 x 1/2"
brown paper
masking tape
1 batch dough
2 batches royal icing
paste food color
liquid food color (green)
Golden Grahams® cereal
2 candy sticks
Necco® candy wafers (black, brown, and purple)
spearmint leaves jelly candies
pretzel sticks
licorice gum (Black Jack®)
small cinnamon candies (Red Hots®)
small piece of muslin or fiddler's cloth
3 tablespoons uncooked rice
2 7-ounce packages shredded coconut
1 7-ounce package marzipan

INSTRUCTIONS

1. Cover plywood board according to general instructions (p. 13) and prepare dough according to recipe (p. 12).

2. Cut and bake the following pieces:
COUNTRY STORE
front—1
back—1
side wall—2
roof—2
roof support—1
door—1
side wall of doorway—2
doorway roof—1
awning—1
billboard—1
storekeeper—1
vegetable bin side—2
vegetable bin top—1
vegetable bin front—1

3. Assemble walls as per general instructions (p. 13).

4. Attach roof support on the back side of the front wall so that the peak corresponds with the peak of the back wall.

5. Attach front door sections.

6. Attach the roof sections.

7. Shingle the roof with Golden Grahams® cereal pieces or material of your choice (p. 16).

8. For store awning, color 1/4 cup royal icing dark green and thin slightly with a few drops of water. Color 2 tablespoons icing chocolate brown and thin slightly. Completely cover the top side of the awning with green icing. While the icing is still wet, pipe thin brown lines perpendicular to the long edge. Set aside to dry.

9. Outline all the features of the storekeeper with brown icing. Using the flood work method (p. 18), ice the various areas with colors desired. Pipe facial features into wet icing. Let dry.

10. Using the same flood method, ice the billboard according to the pattern—blue for sky, green for hills, and yellow for sun. Pipe the lettering in brown after the icing has dried. Set aside.

11. Using white icing, pipe the sugar work signs for the windows on baking parchment. Let dry.

12. Make three spade shovels (p. 20).

13. To make a ladder, use two long pretzel sticks. Cut seven or eight ladder rungs about 1" long out of pretzels. Make sure they are equal in length. Attach all rungs to one side of the ladder first with a dab of icing. Complete the second side. Let dry.

14. Feed bags are made of small scraps of muslin or fiddler's cloth. Cut two rectangles approximately 2 x 3". Stitch around two long sides and one short side about 1/4" from edge. Turn right side out. Create your label with a felt tip pen. Fill with rice and stitch top closed. Wrap thread around each corner to create "ears."

15. To make tomatoes, color a small piece of marzipan red. Break off small bits and roll into balls the size of a pea. Stick a small bit of parsley in the top. Color a walnut-sized ball of marzipan green for heads of lettuce. Break off pieces about 1/2" in diameter and roll. Break

Walden
COUNTRY STORE

STOREKEEPER
cut 1

COUNTRY STORE FRONT
cut 1

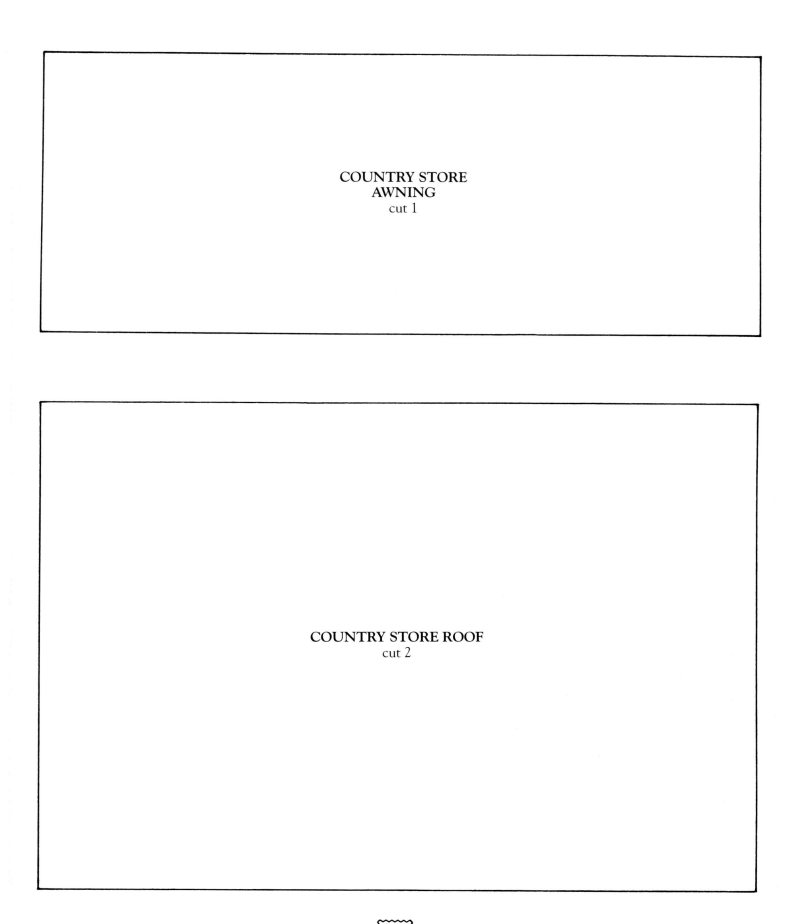

**COUNTRY STORE
AWNING**
cut 1

COUNTRY STORE ROOF
cut 2

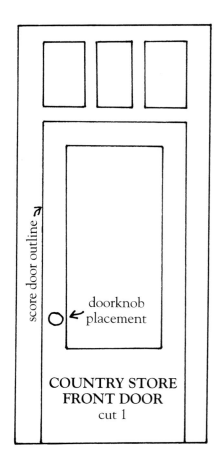

VEGETABLE BIN FRONT
cut 1

VEGETABLE BIN TOP
cut 1

VEG
BIN SIDE
cut 2

score door outline

doorknob
placement

COUNTRY STORE
FRONT DOOR
cut 1

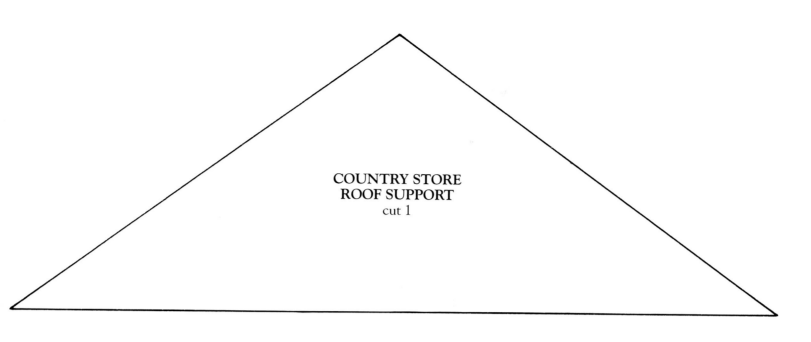

**COUNTRY STORE
ROOF SUPPORT**
cut 1

**COUNTRY STORE
DOORWAY ROOF**
cut 1

off small pieces, flatten into leaves and attach. For carrots, color a small amount of marzipan orange. Roll into carrot shapes. Attach sprigs of parsley for the tops. Make potatoes by dusting pea-sized bits of marzipan into a dish of cocoa powder.

16. Cats may also be created from uncolored marzipan. Roll an egg shape for the 1"-tall body. Flatten the bottom so it will sit. Roll a small piece for the head. Pinch up small bits on either side of the top for the ears. Place a toothpick into the center of the body and attach the head. Using tweezers, fasten two green nonpareils into the face for eyes. Roll small bits of marzipan for feet, two in front and one on each side. Roll a longer piece for tail and attach to fanny area. Paint on stripes with brown paste food coloring. Set aside.

17. Make the walkway (p. 21). Use Necco® wafers or the material of your choice.

18. Build the vegetable bin. Place in front of window. Fill the bottom of bin with potatoes. Attach the remaining vegetables on top with icing.

19. Pipe decorative beading across the front top edges of store and set in Red Hots® candies.

20. Using a #2 writing pastry tip, pipe store name on the storefront.

21. Carefully pipe white icing on the back of the window signs. Place on window mullions.

22. About 1/4" above the windows, pipe a large bead of icing using a star pastry tip in a straight line. Let dry. Cut two candy sticks about 4 1/4" tall. Pipe another line of icing on top of the first. (It will help to have some assistance with the following.) Pipe a dab of icing onto both ends of each candy stick. Place the awning on the wet icing on the face of the building. Slip the candy sticks under the two front corners as support posts. Let dry.

23. Set storekeeper in place by piping a bit of icing on his left arm and feet.

24. Place cat in front of storekeeper.

25. Attach billboard to side of building with icing.

26. Lean the feed sacks against left window.

27. Lean shovels next to feed sacks.

28. Cover all exposed areas of board with coconut grass (p. 21).

29. Lean ladder up against the building.

**COUNTRY
STORE
SIDE WALL
OF
DOORWAY**
cut 2

**BILLBOARD
(FLOOD WORK ON GINGERBREAD)**

COUNTRY STORE SIDE WALL
cut 2

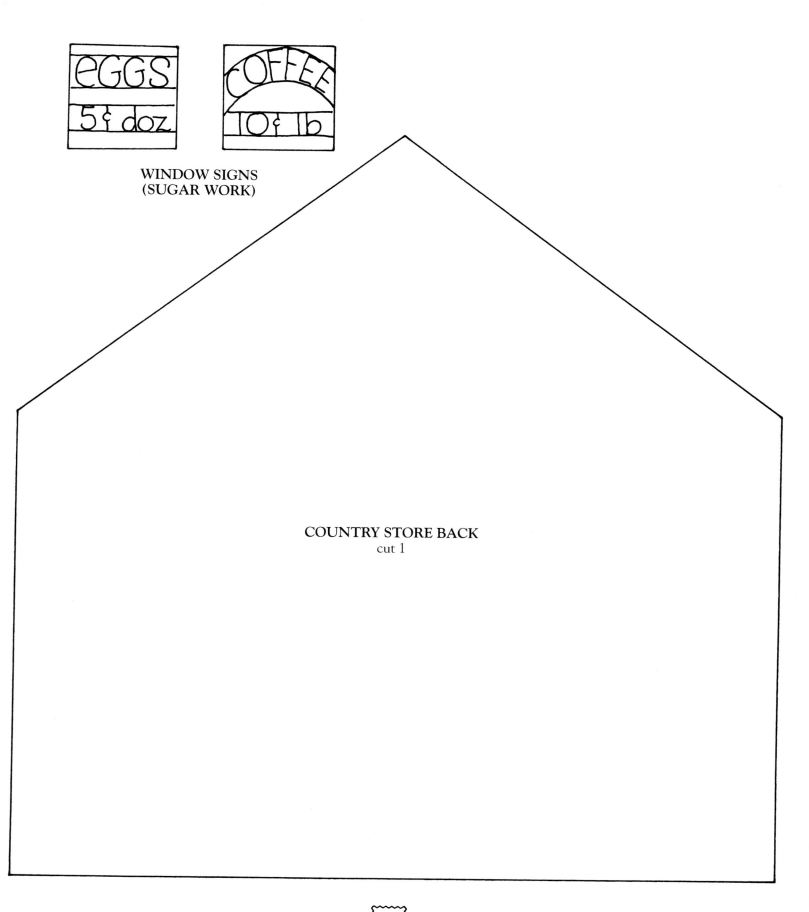

WINDOW SIGNS
(SUGAR WORK)

eGGS
5¢ doz.

COFFEE
10¢ lb

COUNTRY STORE BACK
cut 1

Quilt Shop

THE QUILTS HANGING on the line are a veritable bouquet inspired by nature and by traditional patterns. They were created without a stitch with a palette as colorful as the rainbow.

MATERIALS

plywood board 15 x 27 x 1/2"
brown paper
masking tape
1 batch dough
3 batches royal icing
Bran Chex® cereal
paste food colors
liquid food color (green)
sugar cones (small and large)
2 7-ounce packages shredded coconut
green sugar crystals
1 pound candy pebbles
cocoa powder
2 candy sticks
2 red heart candies
spearmint leaves jelly candies
*straight wire (1/16" TIG wire available in welding
supply stores)*
drill and drill bit (same size as candy sticks)

INSTRUCTIONS

NOTE: For this project, it is best to do all the sugar work the preceding day. See below for quilt instructions.

1. Cover plywood board according to general instructions (p. 13) and prepare dough according to recipe (p. 12).
2. Cut and bake the following pieces:
   QUILT SHOP
   front—1
   back—1 (front with windows, back without)
   side wall—2
   roof—2

3. Decide where your shop will sit on the board and drill holes for clothesline poles in appropriate places.

4. Assemble the shop as per general instructions (p. 13).
5. Place a quilt in the window before attaching the roof.
6. Shingle the roof with Bran Chex® cereal as per instructions (p. 16).
7. Top ridgepole with a row of cinnamon hearts.
8. Pipe all decorative work on walls, around windows and door, including a sign for the shop.
9. Carefully attach peak fancy.
10. Build the stone wall or fence.
11. To make a garden, frost area with brown icing and cover lightly with cocoa powder for soil. Place shrubs in garden if you wish. Carefully remove sugar work flower plants from the parchment and place on the soil.
12. With a dab of icing, attach candy stick clothesline poles into drilled holes in board.
13. Cut stones of different sizes—rounded, oblong, peanut shapes—from licorice gum and set with icing. Leave a bit of room between each stone for grass.
14. Ice the rest of the board a section at a time with green icing and sprinkle with green coconut grass.
15. Pipe a dab of icing on the top of each clothesline pole and lay the clothesline wire across the tops of the posts. Pipe on a bit more icing to hold firm and let dry.
16. Place trees around the shop and hang quilts on the line.

QUILTS AND OTHER SUGAR WORK

NOTE: The icing used to make the quilts is *slightly* less stiff than normal.

1. Begin by slipping the quilt patterns under a piece of parchment. Bend aluminum wire at the bottom corners to correspond with the dotted line on the quilt pattern, making a square U-shape. Leave about 1" above the top edge line on each end of the wire. Curl these ends into small hooks. Make sure the wire quilt frame lays flat against a surface. If not, the quilt will not hang correctly, and it will be nearly impossible to make.
2. Pipe the outline edges of the quilt first and fill in the first border with icing. Lay the wire frame over the dotted line.
3. Overpipe the entire border with approximately two more layers of icing, completely covering the wire

**QUILT SHOP PEAK FANCY
(SUGAR WORK)**

**QUILT SHOP
FRONT AND BACK**
cut front with windows, back without

The Quilting Bee

score door outline

wire

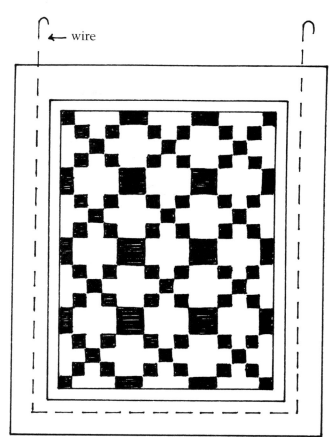

wire

wire

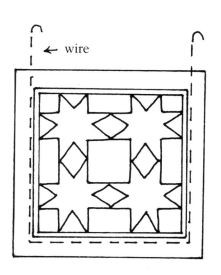

wire

**QUILTS
(SUGAR WORK)**

except where the hooked ends extend beyond the top of the quilt.

4. Pipe in the second border with the desired icing color. Next, pipe in the design of the quilt. Use a toothpick or a very sharp pointed knife to make sure the icing colors get into the corners completely.

5. Fill in the background color. Again, use a toothpick to fill all corners.

6. You may now slip the pattern out from under the parchment and use it as a guide to make any surface decorations such as vine borders, flowers, etc.

7. Make as many quilts as you like, just remember to count the one in the window. To stand the window quilt up, cut two triangles of baked gingerbread or foam core board. Attach them to the back of the quilt and let them dry thoroughly.

8. Pipe the peak fancy for the shop and let dry overnight.

9. Make trees and let dry overnight.

10. Pipe small flower plants for the garden (see carousel instructions p. 103). You will need eighteen small plants and three large. The blossoms are sugar sequins.

11. The next day when the quilts are dry, carefully cut the parchment around the quilts with an X-acto® or craft knife. Leave the parchment on the back for increased durability.

QUILT SHOP SIDE WALL
cut 2

QUILT SHOP ROOF
cut 2

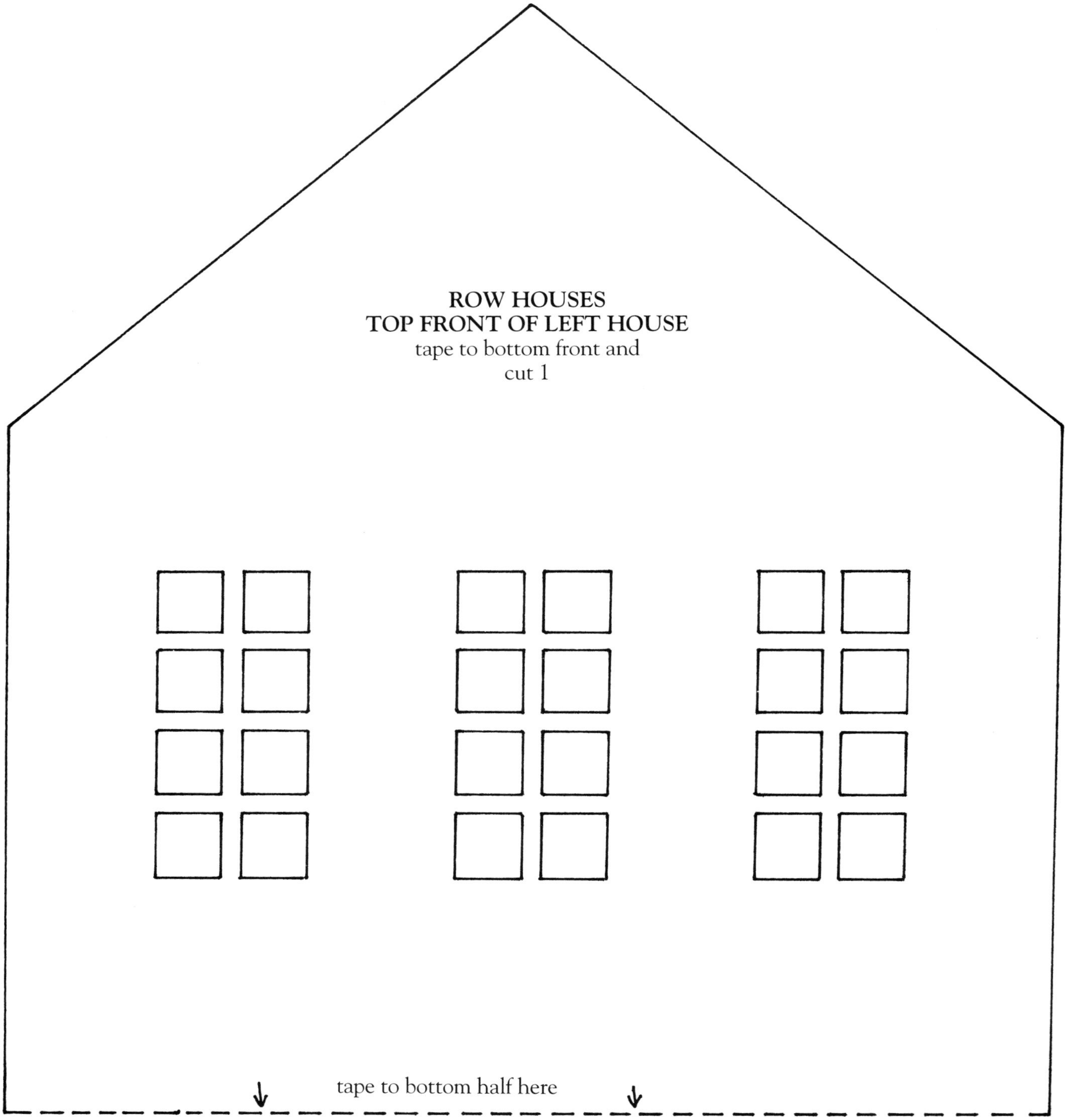

ROW HOUSES
TOP FRONT OF LEFT HOUSE
tape to bottom front and
cut 1

tape to bottom half here

ROW HOUSES

THE CHARM OF these row houses is in keeping with the gentle vision of holiday memories wherever we live. In our imagination, the city and the village blend without difficulty.

MATERIALS

plywood board 15 x 27 x 1/2"
brown paper
masking tape
2 batches dough
2 batches royal icing
Necco® candy wafers (pink, green, yellow, black, brown, and purple)
lace for curtains
1/4 cup sliced almonds
spearmint leaves jelly candies
2 candy sticks
4 large yellow jelly candies (BRACH®'s Fruit Bunch®)
sugar sequins (green)
nonpareils (red)
1 1/2 x 12" sheet of 1/2" Styrofoam® (steps)
drill and drill bit (same size as candy sticks)
votive candle in candle holder (optional)

INSTRUCTIONS

1. Cover plywood board according to general instructions (p. 13) and prepare dough according to recipe (p. 12).
2. Cut out and bake the following pieces:
ROW HOUSES
front—3 (each with a different window style)
back—3
far left wall—1
interior wall—2 (without windows)
far right wall—1
far left roof—1
far right roof—1
center roof—4
porch side wall—3
porch floor—3
porch ceiling—3
front door wall—3
bay window wall—9
bay window roof—9
porch floor support (hidden)—3

NOTE: You will want to attach bits of lace with icing to the inside of the windows before assembly. Pipe all decorative sugar work and set aside to dry.

3. Assemble the houses as per general instructions (p. 13). This structure is unusual as it contains interior walls. Treat these as you would outside walls. Carefully drill holes for lamp posts at this time.
4. Shingle each roof with a different color Necco® candy wafer. You might follow the photograph using green for the first house, pink for the second, and yellow for the third.
5. Shingle the bay window roofs with sliced almonds.
6. Pipe decorations on walls, over windows, and doors.
7. Pipe beading over wall seams and roof edges.
8. Cut 1/2" Styrofoam® into graduated lengths for stairs—three each of 3 x 3", 2 x 3", and 1 x 3". Attach these together. One of each size to make 1 set of stairs. Put each set in place in front of each porch with icing.
9. Cover steps with broken Necco® candy wafers in black, brown, and purple to simulate slate.
10. Make the walkway in the same fashion.
11. Make garlands (p. 19).
12. Make wreaths (p. 19).
13. Make lamp posts and attach firmly in drilled holes.
14. Frost board with icing to create snow.
15. Place spearmint leaf shrubs where desired.
16. *Carefully* attach peak fancies.
17. Pipe a bead using a star tip along the front row edges of roofs.

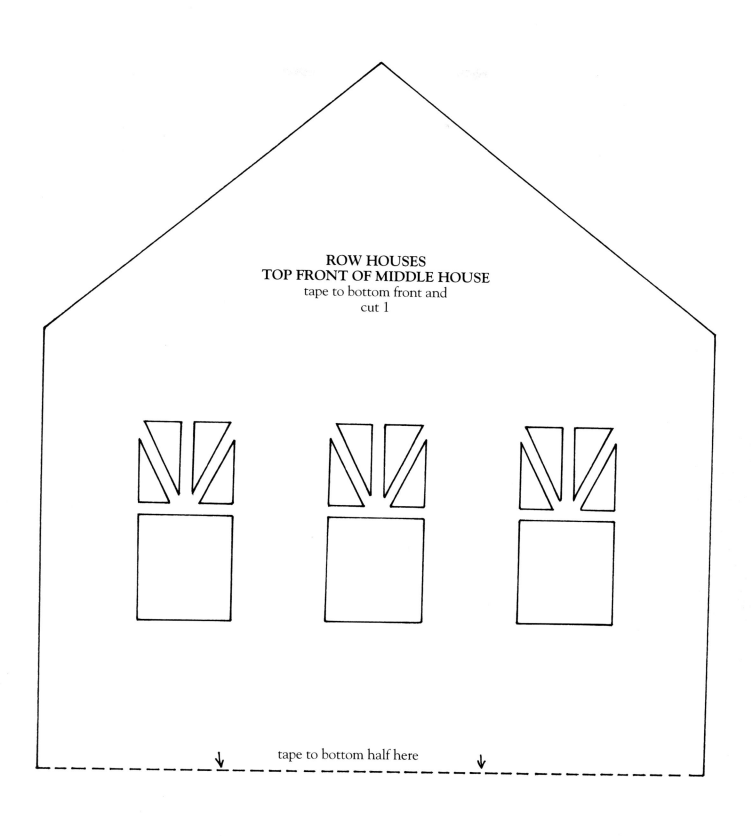

ROW HOUSES
TOP FRONT OF MIDDLE HOUSE
tape to bottom front and
cut 1

tape to bottom half here

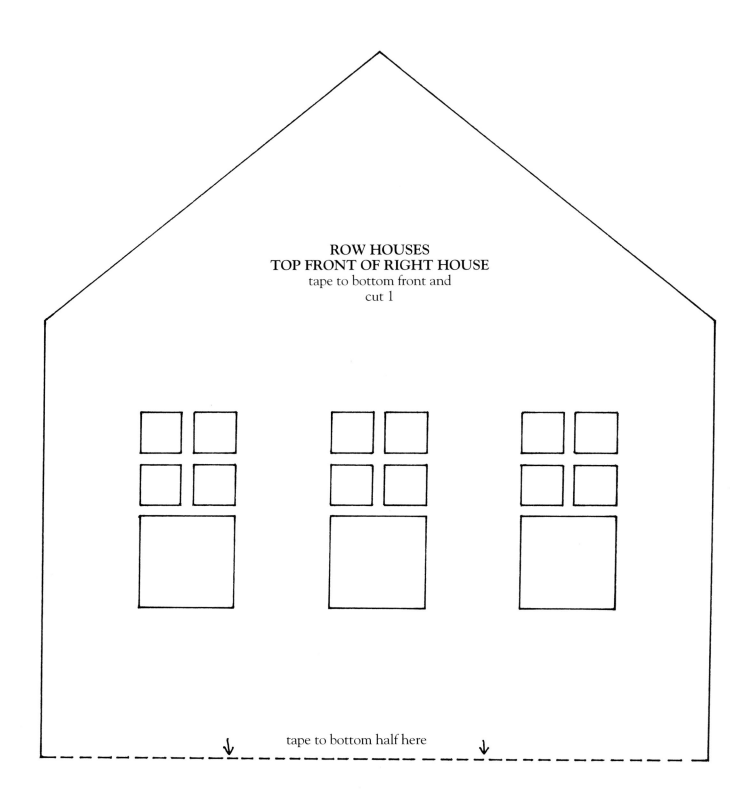

ROW HOUSES
TOP FRONT OF RIGHT HOUSE
tape to bottom front and
cut 1

tape to bottom half here

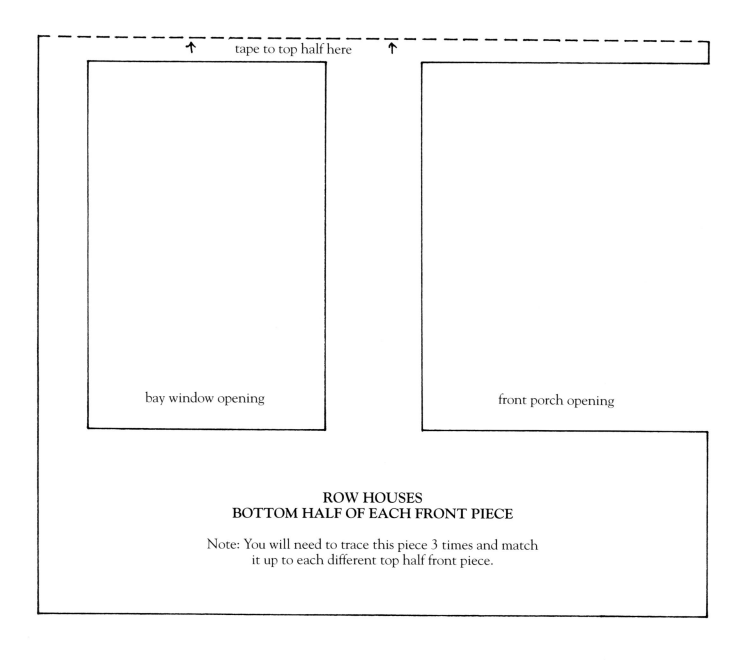

tape to top half here

bay window opening

front porch opening

ROW HOUSES
BOTTOM HALF OF EACH FRONT PIECE

Note: You will need to trace this piece 3 times and match
it up to each different top half front piece.

tape here to top peak of Row Houses back

ROW HOUSES BACK
cut 3

tape here to top peak of Row Houses back

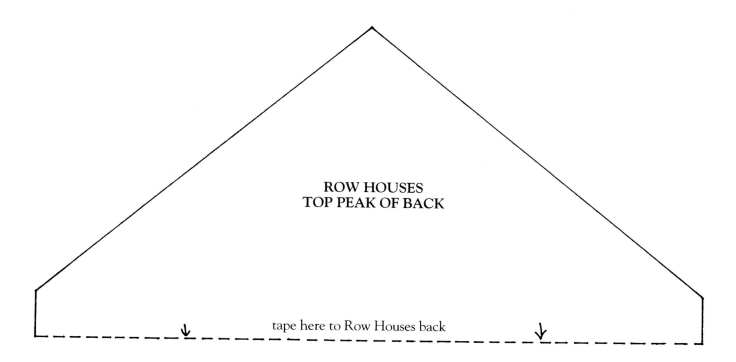

**ROW HOUSES
TOP PEAK OF BACK**

tape here to Row Houses back

ROW HOUSES SIDE WALLS
tape bottom half to top half and cut
2 exterior walls with windows
2 interior walls without windows

tape here to bottom half of side wall

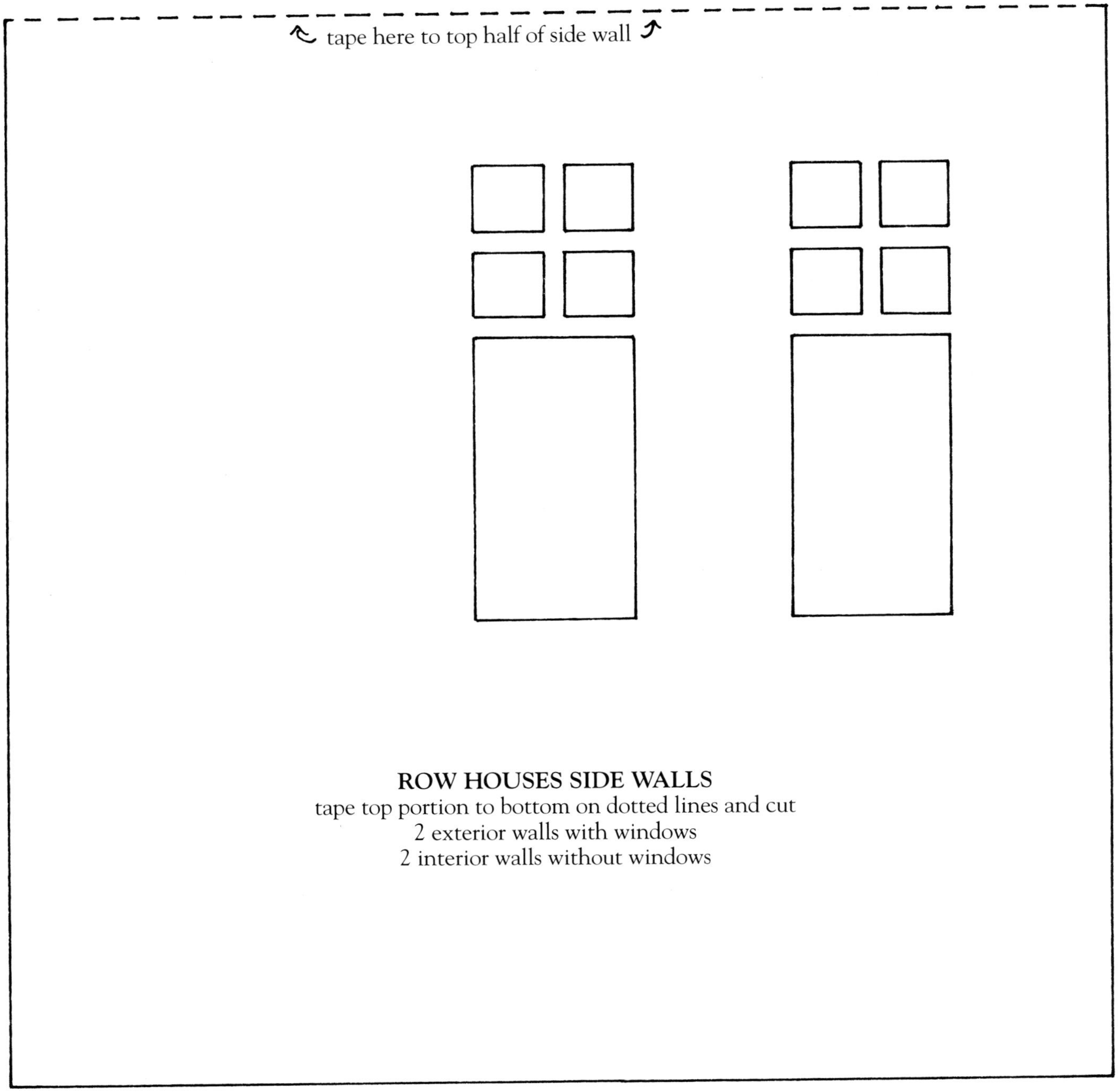

⌒ tape here to top half of side wall ↰

ROW HOUSES SIDE WALLS
tape top portion to bottom on dotted lines and cut
2 exterior walls with windows
2 interior walls without windows

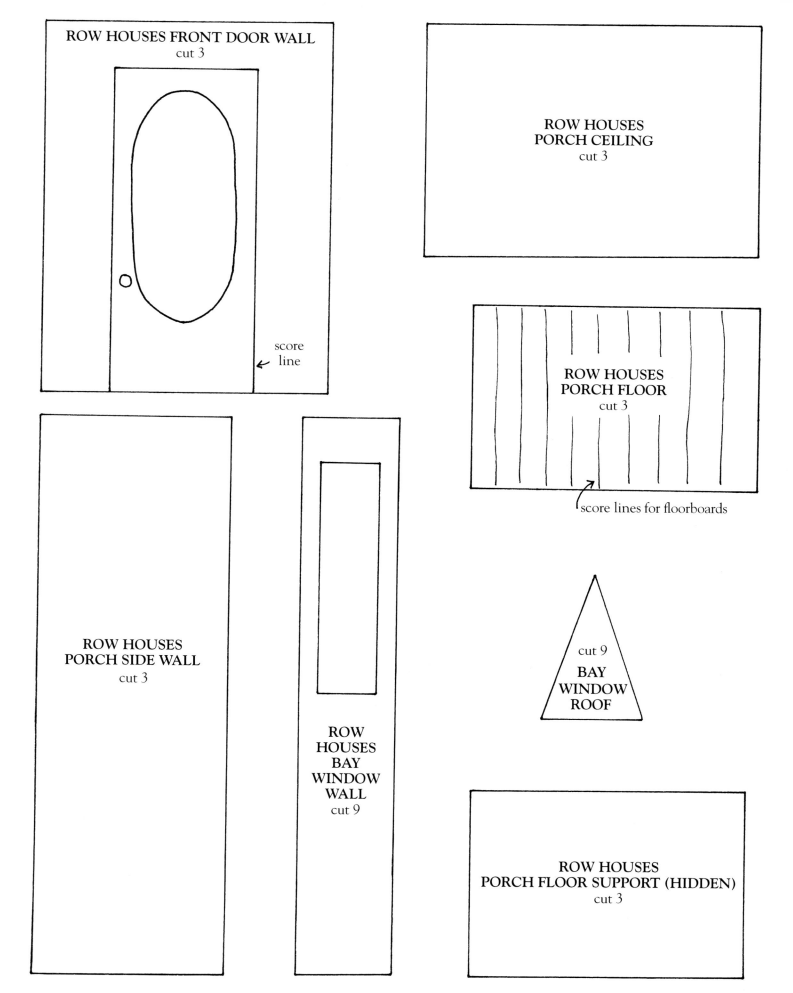

ROW HOUSES FRONT DOOR WALL
cut 3

score line

ROW HOUSES
PORCH CEILING
cut 3

ROW HOUSES
PORCH FLOOR
cut 3

score lines for floorboards

ROW HOUSES
PORCH SIDE WALL
cut 3

ROW HOUSES
BAY WINDOW WALL
cut 9

cut 9
BAY WINDOW ROOF

ROW HOUSES
PORCH FLOOR SUPPORT (HIDDEN)
cut 3

ROW HOUSES CENTER ROOF
cut 4

ROW HOUSES FAR LEFT AND FAR RIGHT
ROOF
cut 2

ROW HOUSES PORCH DECORATIONS

Note: Pipe these designs directly onto
baked gingerbread over porches
before assembling.

LEFT HOUSE

MIDDLE HOUSE

RIGHT HOUSE

PEAK FANCY
LEFT HOUSE

ROW HOUSES
(SUGAR WORK)

PEAK FANCY
MIDDLE HOUSE

PEAK FANCY
RIGHT HOUSE

MILL

A **MILL IS ESSENTIAL** to the life of an expanding village. Situated on a river, our mill runs on water—one of the finest of natural powers.

MATERIALS

plywood board 22 x 22 x 1/2"
1 large sheet 1/4" foam core board
aluminum foil
brown paper
masking tape
36 feet metallic blue curling ribbon
clear tape
1 batch dough
2 batches royal icing
Triscuit Bits®
Triscuits®
sugar sequins (green)
nonpareils (red)
gumdrops (red)
spearmint leaves jelly candies
pretzel sticks
Necco® candy wafers (black, brown, and purple)
1/2 pound candy pebbles
sugar cones (small and large)
green sugar crystals
chocolate sprinkles
1" section of candy stick
8 to 10 pieces Cracklin' Oat Bran® cereal

INSTRUCTIONS

1. Cover plywood board according to general instructions (p. 13) and prepare dough according to recipe (p. 12).

2. Cut out and bake the following pieces:

MILL
front—1
back—1 (front with windows, back without)
large side wall—2
small side wall—8 (6 with windows, 2 without)
main roof—2
gable roof—4 (2 with pattern face up, 2 face down)
cupola side wall—4
cupola roof—4
cap (under roof)—1
wheel—2 (1 with pattern face up, 1 face down)

3. Draw the positions of the building and stream on the board.

4. Cover the stream area with foil and secure in place. It does not have to be contoured as the actual stream will be.

5. Since the mill sits up on a hill, it is necessary to build up this area with 1/4" foam core board in graduated pieces. The first piece you cut will be the top of the hill where the mill sits. Use an X-acto® or craft knife to cut the board and round the edges.

6. Cut two more pieces in graduated sizes making sure that the bank side stays vertical.

7. Cut three pieces of foam core board for the other bank in the same manner. Glue all pieces down with rubber cement.

8. Assemble the mill on top of the hill as per general instructions (p. 13). Make sure the mill wheel wall is close to the cliff.

9. Shingle the roof with Triscuit Bits®. The cupola is covered with standard-size Triscuits® cut to fit.

10. Make garlands (p. 19) over the Palladian window and under two small windows in front.

11. Pipe decorative bead of icing over wall seams.

12. Pipe any decorative icing you desire over and under windows.

13. Attach silver dragées for doorknobs.

14. To make the mill wheel, lay one wheel piece smooth side down. At each spoke attach one piece of Cracklin' Oat Bran® cereal with a dab of icing. When that step is completed, dab icing on the tops of each cereal piece and attach the other mill wheel smooth side up. Set aside to dry.

15. Make seven rail fence sections (p. 20). Set aside to dry.

16. Make trees (p. 19).

17. Build a stone retaining wall on banks of river using candy pebbles and icing.

18. Frost the hills with white icing. Be generous with

MILL FRONT AND BACK
cut front with windows, back without

← score door lines

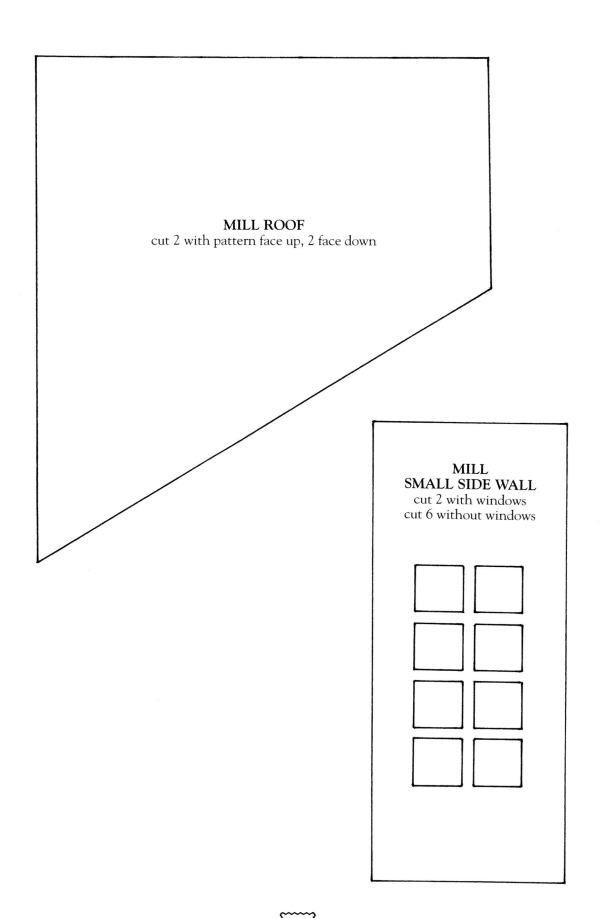

MILL ROOF
cut 2 with pattern face up, 2 face down

**MILL
SMALL SIDE WALL**
cut 2 with windows
cut 6 without windows

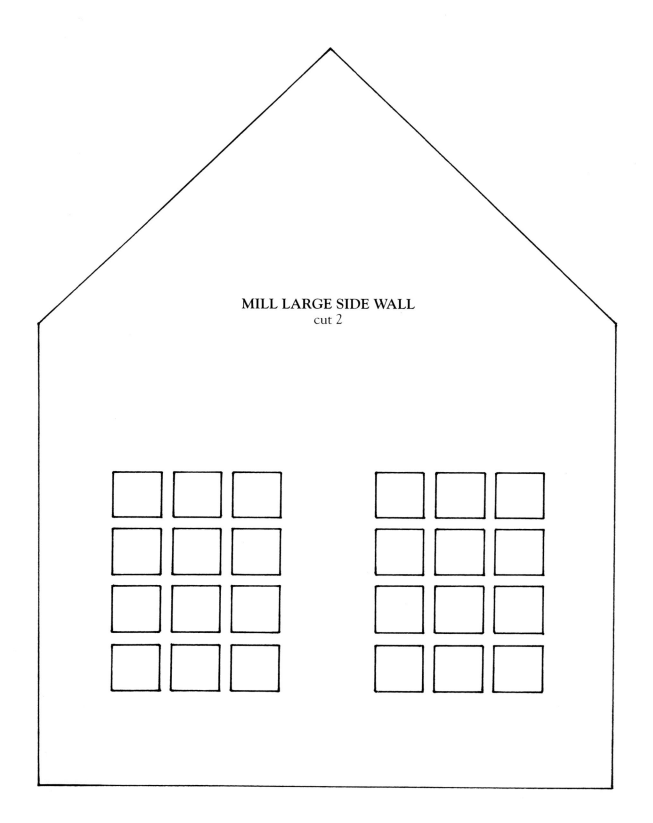

MILL LARGE SIDE WALL
cut 2

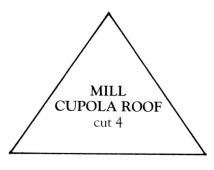

**MILL
CUPOLA ROOF**
cut 4

**MILL CAP
(UNDER ROOF)**
cut 1

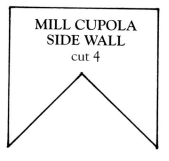

**MILL CUPOLA
SIDE WALL**
cut 4

the icing on the slopes, making sure you cover the foam core board.

19. Make your walkway out of broken Necco® candy wafers.

20. Set spearmint leaf shrubs in place.

21. Set trees in place.

22. Stand up fence sections.

23. Cut about 36 one-foot lengths of blue, metallic curling ribbon. Curl each piece, some tightly, others more loosely. Using pieces of clear tape the width of the river, attach one end of each ribbon side by side across the tape (blue side of ribbon should stick to tape).

24. Beginning approximately 2" from the front of the board, stick a streamer-tape to the riverbed. Make sure the streamers fall forward. Repeat this process 2" farther upstream. These ribbons will hide the preceding piece of tape. Continue in this manner until the entire river is covered.

25. Cut a 1" piece of candy stick. This will be the mill axle.

26. With icing, glue the candy stick to the lower middle section of river side mill wall. Attach mill wheel to candy stick with icing.

27. You may speckle crushed chocolate sprinkles on the far bank as dirt.

MILL WHEEL
cut 1 with pattern face up, 1 face down

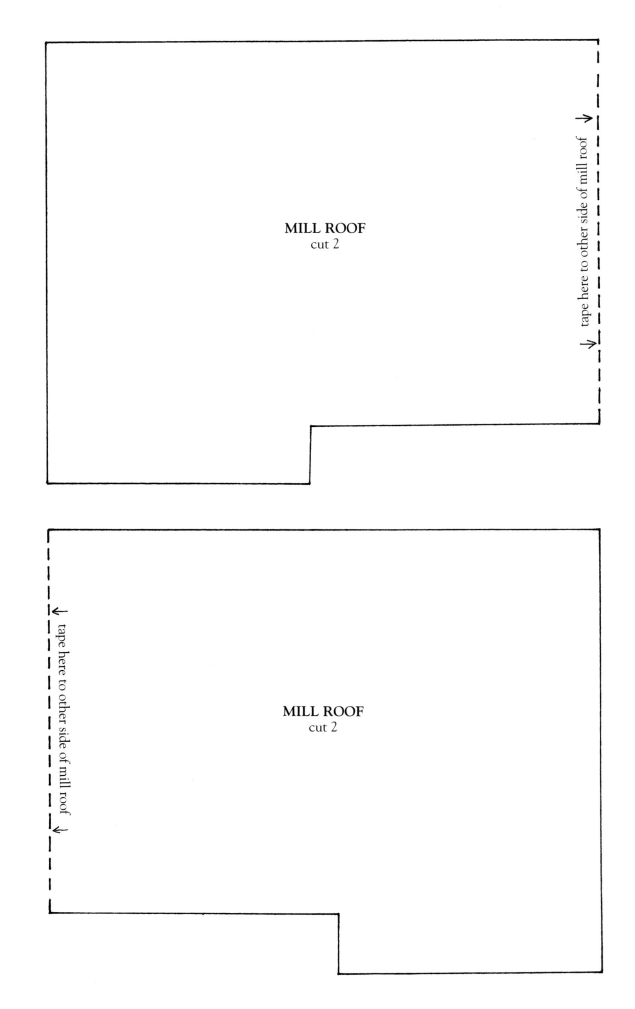

MILL ROOF
cut 2

tape here to other side of mill roof

MILL ROOF
cut 2

tape here to other side of mill roof

CHURCH

IN THE CENTER of our village stands the church, the spiritual and religious center. Its steeple reaches toward the sky and its stained glass windows glow with light, as the townspeople gather to pray.

MATERIALS

plywood board 15 x 15 x 1/2"
brown paper
masking tape
aluminum foil
1 batch dough
2 batches royal icing
1 sugar cone for the steeple
sliced almonds
18 ounces semisweet chocolate chips
hard candies in several colors (sour balls, Lifesavers®, crystal mints)
Necco® candy wafers (black, brown, and purple)
1/2" Styrofoam®
sugar sequins (green)
nonpareils (red)
4 jumbo candy canes
spearmint leaves jelly candies
votive candle in candle holder (optional)

INSTRUCTIONS

1. Cover plywood board according to general instructions (p. 13) and prepare dough according to recipe (p. 12).

2. Cut out and bake the following pieces:
CHURCH
front—1
back—1 (cut front with windows, back without)
*side wall—2 (cut 2 9" wide and 10" high)**
main roof—2
front pediment—1
clock tower front—1
clock tower back—1
clock tower side—2
clock tower roof—1
bell tower wall—4
bell tower roof—1

*Because you will be creating stained glass windows for the side pieces, there is a slightly different method for preparation. Roll and cut the dough out on aluminum foil so the stained glass candy work will not stick. Bake these sections two-thirds of the required baking time. Remove from oven and place crushed colored hard candies such as sour balls, Lifesavers®, or crystal mints into the divisions. Be sure to brush any candy off the surface of the gingerbread as it will make a sticky spot. Finish baking, but make sure the candy does not over bake and caramelize. The candies will melt creating the windows. Let cool *completely* before removing the foil.

3. Assemble the main building as per general instructions (p. 13).

4. Assemble the clock section of the tower upside down and set aside to dry.

5. Assemble the bell tower in the same fashion.

6. Shape a bell out of aluminum foil and attach it to the roof of the bell tower with a dab of icing. Set aside to dry.

7. Shingle a sugar cone with sliced almonds.

8. Pipe the sugar work and set aside to dry.

9. The clock is created by icing a Necco® candy wafer and placing purple colored sprinkles on the face. Use tweezers. The hands are chocolate sprinkles. Set aside to dry.

10. Create steps by making a foundation with Styrofoam®. You will need a small sheet of 1/2" Styrofoam®. Cut the bottom step 9 x 3 1/2". Cut the top step 9 x 2 1/2".

11. Attach the bottom step with icing. Center the top step above the first and attach with icing.

12. Cover the tops and sides of the steps with broken Necco® candy wafers as you would for a walkway.

13. Pipe a bead of icing along all step edges.

14. Decorate the church with swags of garland under the windows. Pipe any window decorations you desire. Pipe a beaded line around the door and attach dragée doorknobs.

15. Measure the vertical distance between the top of the stairs and the bottom of the front pediment. Cut four jumbo candy canes to this length. Put in place with icing.

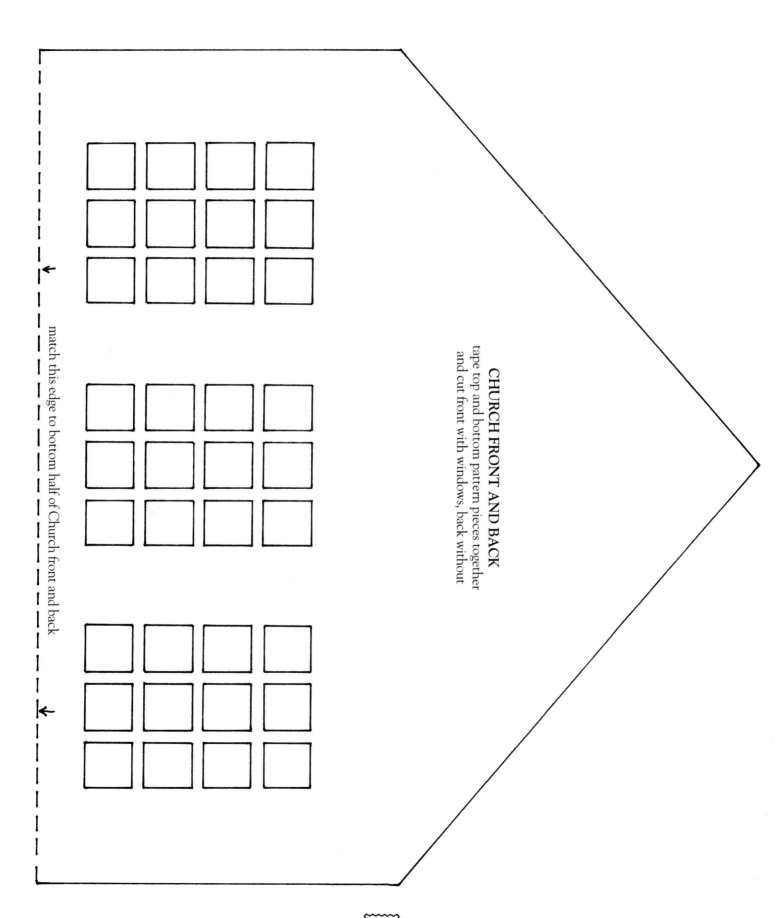

CHURCH FRONT AND BACK
tape top and bottom pattern pieces together and cut front with windows, back without

match this edge to bottom half of Church front and back

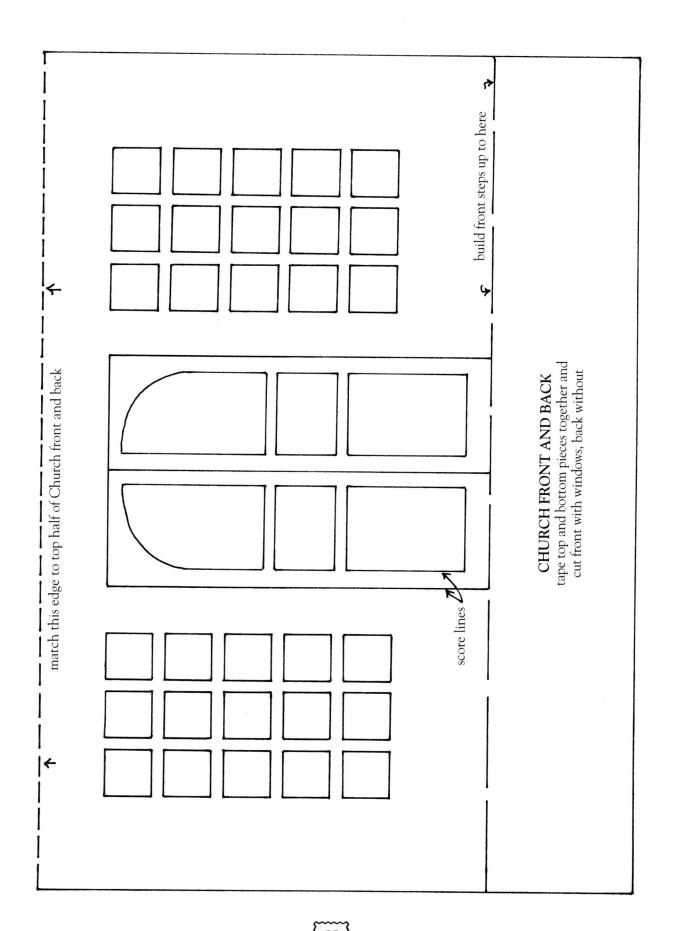

match this edge to top half of Church front and back

build front steps up to here

CHURCH FRONT AND BACK
tape top and bottom pieces together and
cut front with windows, back without

score lines

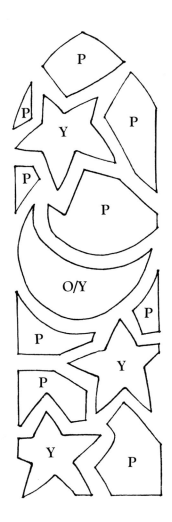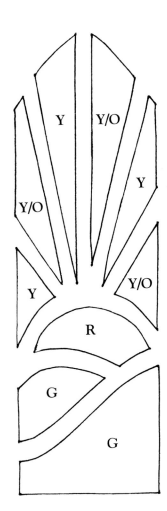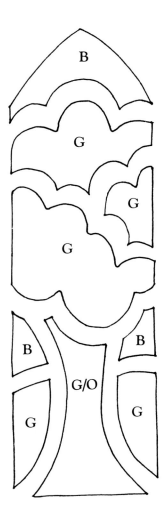

CHURCH SIDE WALL WINDOWS

Note: Cut 2 CHURCH SIDE WALLS 9" wide by 10" high.
Place and cut window patterns in center of wall.

R=Red O=Orange Y=Yellow G=Green B=Blue P=Purple

16. Attach clock section of the tower in place with icing.

17. Attach bell tower to top of clock section.

18. Attach steeple.

19. Shingle the roof with chocolate shingles (p. 16).

20. Using a star pastry tip, pipe decorative beading along wall seams and roof edges. Carefully place arched window in front pediment.

21. Attach clock to tower with a dab of icing.

22. Place a dab of icing on the top of steeple and very carefully attach weathervane.

23. Frost the board to simulate snow.

24. Landscape as desired with trees and shrubbery.

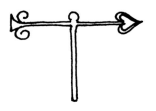

CHURCH WEATHERVANE (SUGAR WORK)
make 1

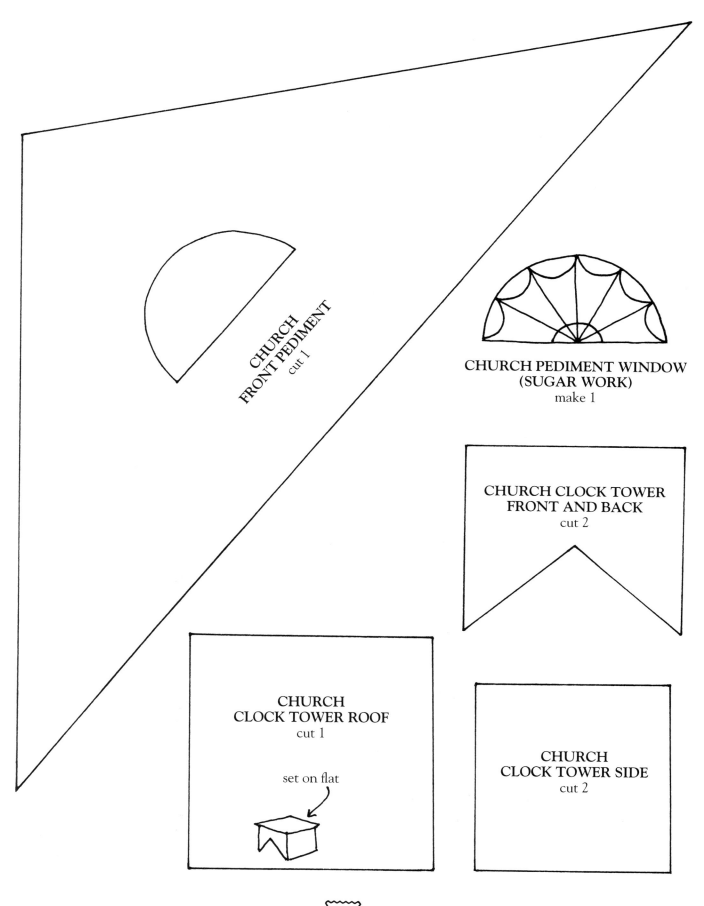

CHURCH
FRONT PEDIMENT
cut 1

CHURCH PEDIMENT WINDOW
(SUGAR WORK)
make 1

CHURCH CLOCK TOWER
FRONT AND BACK
cut 2

CHURCH
CLOCK TOWER ROOF
cut 1

set on flat

CHURCH
CLOCK TOWER SIDE
cut 2

**CHURCH
BELL TOWER ROOF**
cut 1
place steeple on top

**CHURCH
BELL TOWER
SIDE**
cut 4

CHURCH MAIN ROOF
tape pattern pieces together and cut 2

tape here to other half of roof

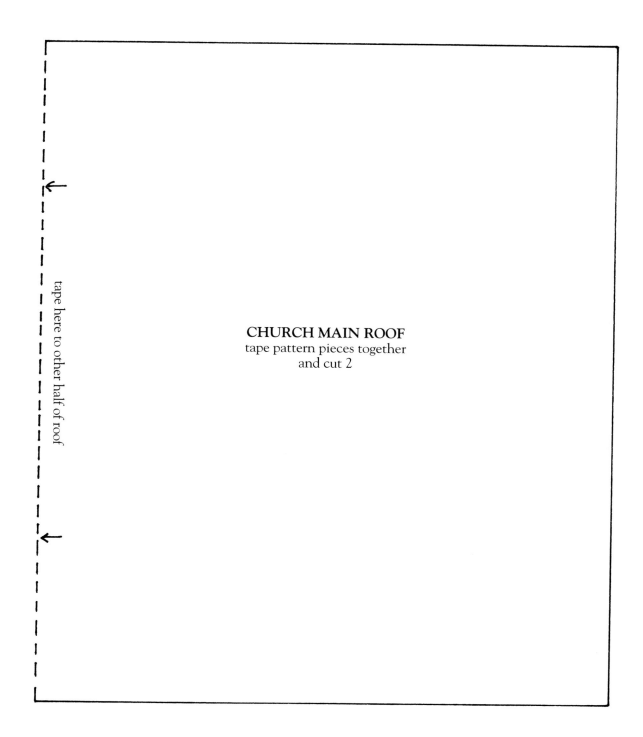

CHURCH MAIN ROOF
tape pattern pieces together
and cut 2

tape here to other half of roof

CAROUSEL

ONE CAN ALMOST hear the sound of the calliope playing as children happily ride the prancing ponies.

MATERIALS

plywood board 15 x 15 x 1/2"
brown paper
masking tape
1 batch dough
2 batches royal icing
1 7-ounce package shredded coconut
paste food colors
liquid food color (green)
nonpareils (assorted)
Smarties®
sugar sequins (red)
green sugar crystals
sugar cones (small and large)
4 candy sticks at least 4 1/2" long
cardboard tube (1 1/2–2" diameter)

INSTRUCTIONS

NOTE: It is helpful to place the board on a lazy Susan so it may be turned easily while you work on all sides of the carousel.

1. Cover plywood board according to general instructions (p. 13) and prepare dough according to recipe (p. 12).

2. Cut and bake the following pieces:
CAROUSEL
base—1
ceiling (under roof)—1
side section—8
roof section—8

3. Pipe all sugar work first on parchment as per directions (p. 17). Use patterns given for horses and fence sections. Pipe extra roof decorations because it is probable that several will break. Allow to dry overnight.

4. Assemble the sections of the carousel first and then attach them to the board instead of building directly on the board as with the other buildings. Set the carousel base smooth side down on a cookie sheet. Using a #6 writing pastry tip, pipe icing around three sides of the octagonal shape.

5. Pipe a bead of icing on both short ends of one side piece. Attach this piece to the center section of the three sides of the base on which you piped icing.

6. Attach one side piece to each side of the first attached. Work your way around the base attaching the base pieces to each other and to the base until the octagon is complete. Pipe reinforcing icing on the inside seams. Let dry.

7. Place the other octagonal piece (under roof) smooth side down on the cookie sheet. In the same manner as the base, pipe icing on three edges of the octagon and on the edges of one roof triangle.

8. Attach this roof triangle to the center iced edge of the under roof octagon. Add another one on each side of the first. Work your way around bringing all the triangle points together at the center. You may need to trim the last piece to fit. Do so with a serrated knife using a sawing motion. Use little pressure as the gingerbread is very fragile. Let dry thoroughly.

9. Cut a length of cardboard tube 4 1/2" long. You may use paper towel or wrapping paper tubes. Cover this

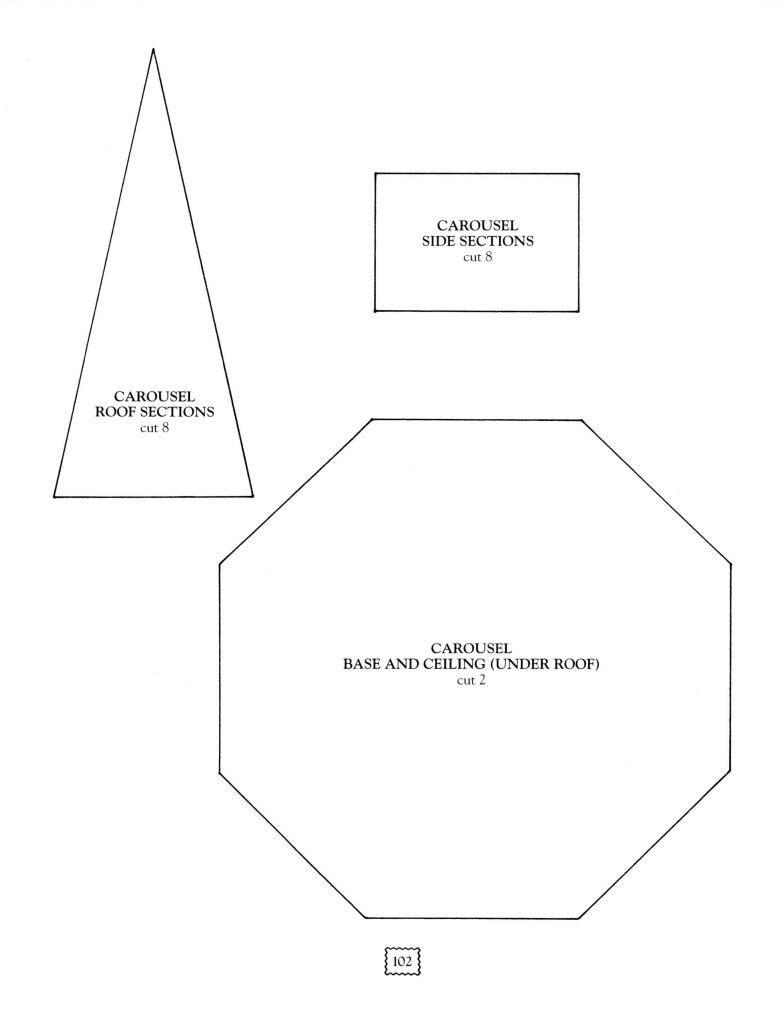

CAROUSEL
SIDE SECTIONS
cut 8

CAROUSEL
ROOF SECTIONS
cut 8

CAROUSEL
BASE AND CEILING (UNDER ROOF)
cut 2

CAROUSEL ROOF FANCIES
(SUGAR WORK)
make 30
(here are 6)

CAROUSEL HORSES
(SUGAR WORK)
make 2 of each

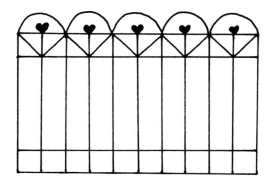

FENCE SECTION
(SUGAR WORK)
make 8 to 10

with icing and decorative candies. We used Smarties® and applied them in a rainbow fashion.

10. Make as many trees as you desire (p. 19).

11. Color about 1/2 cup of royal icing green or use left-overs from tree making. Put this into an icing bag with a #67 leaf pastry tip.

12. On parchment, pipe about forty little plants. These are actually small mounds of icing with leaf tips pointing upward. Add four or five pink sugar sequins to the center of each. Let dry.

13. Using pink icing, pipe small heart designs on each side piece. Let dry.

14. Decide where you want your carousel on the board. We suggest slightly toward the back from center. Pipe icing on the bottom edge of the base and attach to the board.

15. Center candy-covered cardboard tube on the base and attach in place with icing. Let set.

16. Draw your walkway on the board and pave with broken Necco® candy wafers as in general directions (p. 24).

17. Center roof on the cardboard tube and attach with icing.

18. Measure and cut four candy sticks to size so they fit nicely between the base and the under roof. They will be about 4 1/2" long plus or minus any bubbles in the gingerbread.

19. *Carefully* remove your horses from the parchment and pipe reinforcing icing on the back side of each. Let dry.

20. Attach one horse to each candy stick pole using plenty of icing. Let dry. (Use an extra candy stick under the nose of each horse to prop it up while drying.)

21. Carefully attach the horses on poles by icing each end of the candy stick and positioning them evenly around the carousel.

22. Shingle the roof with Smarties®.

23. Pipe decorative beading over all seams using a star pastry tip.

24. Pipe decorative beading around the bottom edge of the roof about two sections at a time and putting the roof decorations into the wet icing.

25. Using brown icing with dry cocoa powder, create your garden along the walkway and "plant" the flowers.

26. Place fence sections carefully with icing between the gardens and walkways.

27. Add grass (p. 21) and position trees.

GINGERBREAD BASKET

MATERIALS

oven-proof bowl approximately 10" in diameter
nonstick cooking spray
1 batch dough
2 yards 1 1/2" double-face-satin ribbon

INSTRUCTIONS

1. Prepare dough according to recipe (p. 12).

2. Invert the bowl on a cookie sheet lined with baking parchment and trace the outline of the bowl on the parchment. Spray the outside of the oven-proof bowl with cooking spray.

3. Taking a softball-sized amount of dough, pat it into a flat, square shape. Roll it out farther to a 1/4" thickness.

4. Cut dough into 1" strips.

5. Carefully lay one strip across the bowl. Make sure it is is long enough to reach the cookie sheet on both sides. Lay another strip perpendicular to the first one across the top to form right angles.

6. Add another strip to each side of the first strip.

7. Add one strip to each side of the second strip, but the two must go over then under the previous strips as in weaving.

8. The last two strips go around the widest part of the basket and it will probably be necessary to join two strips together to make this possible. Pick a starting point and weave over, under, over, and under until you return to your starting point. When you join the pieces,

attach them with a drop or two of water, then press firmly in place.

9. Repeat this process with the second set of strips in the opposite direction but from the same starting point.

10. Trim off the ends at the base of the bowl.

11. Bake until golden brown and let cool about 10 minutes.

12. *Carefully* loosen the basket from its form but do not remove. Let it cool completely on the form.

13. To make the basket rim, measure the circumference of the circle traced on the baking parchment. (It is about 3.2 times the diameter.) Make a rope of gingerbread dough and roll it to approximately 3/8" thick.

14. Cut two strips lengthwise and about 1" wide. Carefully twist the strips over and under each other to create a twisted rope effect.

15. Slide the baking parchment with drawn circle under this rope and curve it around to match the circle. It should be centered on the circle, not to the inside or outside. Trim the ends so they join properly and attach with a drop or two of water.

16. Bake until brown and let cool thoroughly.

17. Remove gingerbread basket from the bowl form. Attach twisted basket rim to the basket body with royal icing. You may color the icing brown if you prefer it to be less noticeable. Let dry.

18. Weave a double-faced 1 1/2" satin ribbon through the basket near the top. Tie a bow.

19. Fill with bread, rolls, Christmas ornaments, Easter eggs, party crackers, miniature pumpkins, or foil-covered chocolate turkeys.

NOAH

LIONESS

LION

ARK (ORNAMENT ONLY)

FLOOD WORK ON GINGERBREAD

Note: If you wish to
use Noah and the animals
as ornaments, be sure
to pierce a hole at the
top of each before baking so they may
be hung up with ribbon.

NOAH'S ARK

THE ANIMALS COME two by two to join Noah in a voyage on his ark. The ark is complete with doves and a rainbow and all are present and accounted for.

MATERIALS

oval plywood board 12 x 18 x 1/2"
brown paper
masking tape
1 batch dough
2 batches royal icing
pretzel sticks
1 pretzel log
red heart candies
paste food colors
shredded Mylar (blue and green)
small paintbrush

INSTRUCTIONS

1. Cover plywood board according to general instructions (p. 13) and prepare dough according to recipe (p. 12).
2. Cut and bake the following pieces:
NOAH'S ARK
side—2
deck support—2
deck—1
bow and stern board—about 24
cabin side wall—2
cabin front wall—1
cabin back wall—1
cabin roof—2
animals—2 each, of course
Noah—1

3. Place the deck smooth side down as we are building upside down. Pipe icing to the sides of the deck and attach side walls.
4. Pipe icing on the deck supports and snug them up against the inside of the side wall where it meets the deck. (It is wise to have a helper at this step.)
5. Pipe icing about 1" down the curved edge of the ark sides beginning from the flat area.
6. Place slats across the distance from one side to the other. Work your way down the curved edges (bow and stern) with slats, icing the curved edge and the long edges of the slats. Let dry overnight.
7. Assemble the ark cabin as per general instructions. Let dry.
8. Pipe icing on the flat edges of the ark bottom and invert, placing it on the board in the desired position.
9. Attach the ark cabin to the deck with icing.
10. Shingle the cabin roof by placing pretzel sticks side by side across the roof. One large pretzel rod cut to size is the ridgepole.
11. Pipe two sugar work doves as per pattern. When dry, attach to the ridgepole with a bit of icing.
12. Pipe a decorative bead of icing using a star tip or a #4 writing pastry tip on all seams.
13. Pipe a decorative bead of icing around the deck edge and set in candy hearts for the railing.
14. Pipe a sugar work rainbow using colored icings. Let dry. When dry, attach rainbow in place on bow of boat.
15. Decorate Noah and the animals using the flood work technique described in the directions (p. 19). When dry attach in place with icing.

NOTE: This centerpiece looks very pretty sitting in a sea of shredded blue and green Mylar (available in craft or party stores).

NOAH'S ARK ANIMALS
(FLOOD WORK ON GINGERBREAD)

TIGER

CAMEL

ELEPHANT

GIRAFFE

HIPPOPOTAMUS

ALLIGATOR

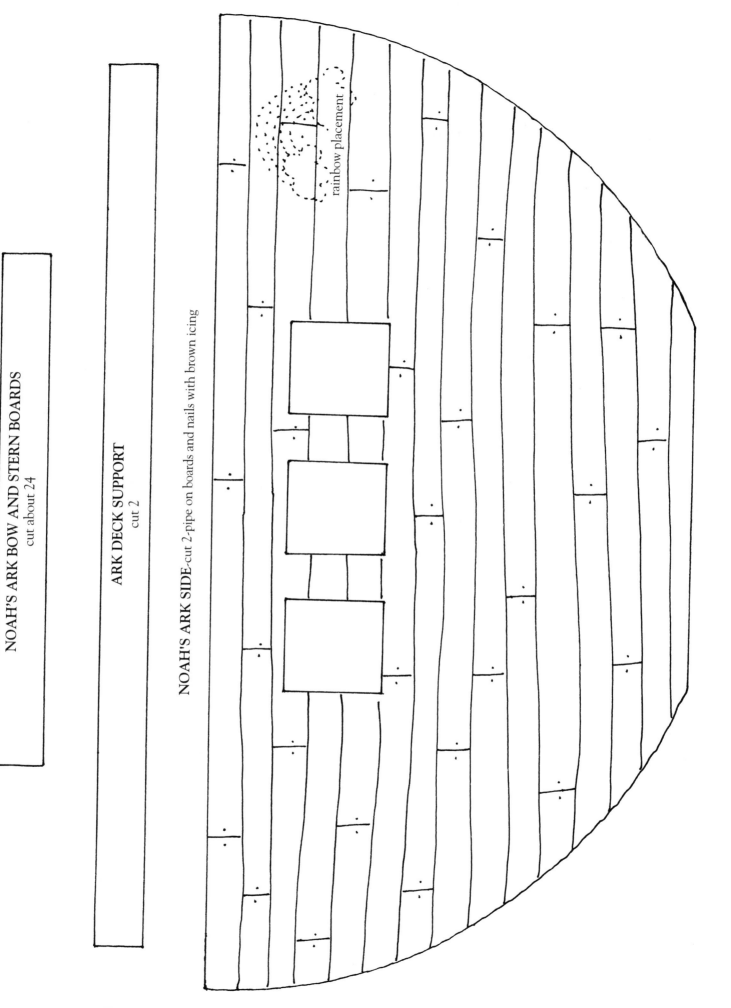

NOAH'S ARK BOW AND STERN BOARDS
cut about 24

ARK DECK SUPPORT
cut 2

NOAH'S ARK SIDE—cut 2-pipe on boards and nails with brown icing

rainbow placement

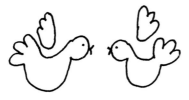

DOVES
(SUGAR WORK)

RAINBOW
(SUGAR WORK)

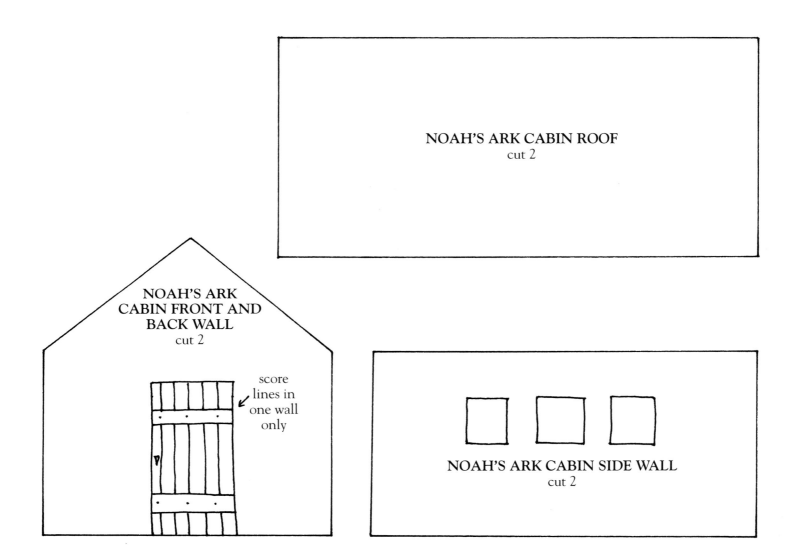

NOAH'S ARK CABIN ROOF
cut 2

NOAH'S ARK
CABIN FRONT AND
BACK WALL
cut 2

score
lines in
one wall
only

NOAH'S ARK CABIN SIDE WALL
cut 2

NOAH'S ARK DECK
cut 1

Angel Mobile

MATERIALS

1 batch dough
6 yards 1/8" silk ribbon
1 batch icing
1 small bunch paper flowers
2 twigs 12" long (1/2" diameter)
6 yards fishing line
paste food colors

INSTRUCTIONS

1. Prepare dough according to recipe (p. 12). Cut out angels and stars. Bake.

2. Tie twigs together with ribbon so they form 90° angles.
3. Ice both sides of angels and stars using flood work technique (p. 18) and pictures as a guide.
4. Attach arms with icing. Attach flowers and ribbon streamers if desired.
5. Tie a piece of fishing line approximately 18–24" long each through holes of angels and stars.
6. Tie one angel to each end of twigs and one to center.
7. Use stars as balance weights where required.

NOTE: Do not hang the mobile directly over a baby's crib because the gingerbread will break off and fall into the crib.

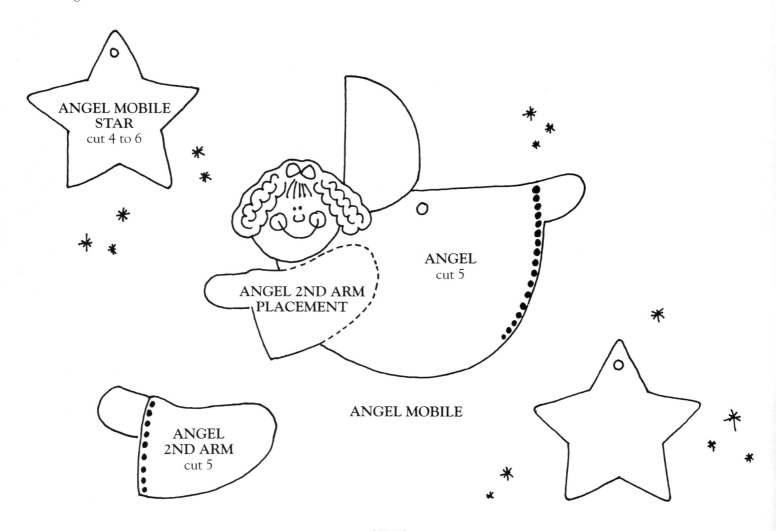

ANGEL MOBILE STAR
cut 4 to 6

ANGEL 2ND ARM PLACEMENT

ANGEL
cut 5

ANGEL 2ND ARM
cut 5

ANGEL MOBILE

TOY WREATH
ORNAMENTS
(FLOOD WORK
ON GINGERBREAD)

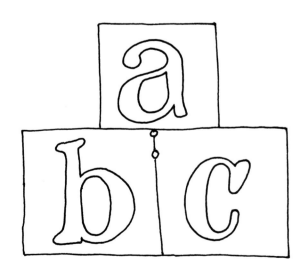

Toy Wreath

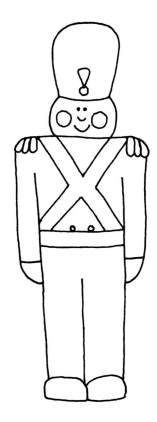

MATERIALS

1 batch dough
manila file folders or oak tag
X-acto® or craft knife
10–12" grape vine wreath
5–6 stems of ivy (silk or real)*
2–3 bunches small red berries
1 spool green florist wire
wire cutters
hot glue gun (optional)

*If real, put each stem in a vial of water

INSTRUCTIONS

1. Prepare dough according to recipe (p. 12).
2. Transfer toy cookie patterns to manila file folders. Cut out using an X-acto® or craft knife.
3. Roll dough on baking parchment. Using patterns, cut into toy shapes with a very sharp knife. Bake.
4. Let cookies cool. Ice each cookie using the flood work technique (p. 18). Refer to the photograph as a guide or use your own imagination.
5. Prepare the wreath by wrapping ivy stems through the center and around the outer edge several times, making sure the water vials (if using real ivy) are to the back. Hold ivy in place with small twists or florist wire. Wrap as many stems around the wreath as you desire.
6. Fasten the cookies to the wreath using florist wire and a hot glue gun (optional). If you decide not to use the glue gun, you can eat the cookies. From the front side, thread the wire through the holes as you would a button, and push the ends of the wire through the wreath. Twist the ends together at the back. Cut off excess wire. Be sure not to pull the wire too tight as there is a chance the cookie could break.
7. Using a hot glue gun or wire twists, fasten red berries to the wreath.
8. Make a wire loop at the back of the wreath for hanging.

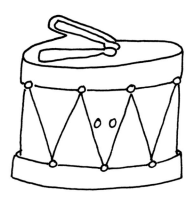

ORNAMENTS

All ornaments are prepared in the same manner, by making a batch of dough and cutting out the patterns using a sharp, thin-blade knife. For any ornament you wish to hang, remember that before you bake you must make a hole in the center at the top large enough to pass a piece of ribbon or string through.

The quilt block ornaments, *scherenschnitte* cutouts, toys for the wreath, and Noah's Ark animals are all decorated by the flood work method. Follow the directions on page 18, coloring in the areas as desired.

The carousel horses and storefronts are piped designs. Use colors of icing as you desire or follow the colors in the photographs in this book.

**CAROUSEL HORSE
ORNAMENT**

SCHERENSCHNITTE
ORNAMENTS

STOREFRONT ORNAMENTS

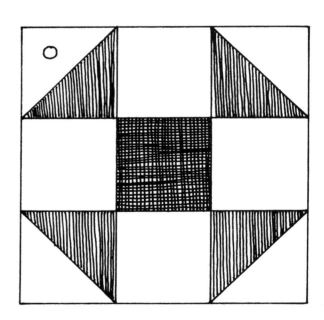

QUILT BLOCK ORNAMENTS

SPINNING STAR
ORNAMENT

SPINNING HEART
ORNAMENT

Sources

The Baker's Find: 139 Woodworth Avenue, Yonkers, NY 10701–2512, (800) 966–BAKE; flours, nuts, decorations, colorings

The Bridge Company: 214 East 52nd Street, New York, NY 10012, (212) 688–4220; baking sheets, pans, utensils, cookie cutters

The Chef's Pantry: P.O. Box 3, Post Mills, VT 05058, (800) TRY–CHEF; condiments and delicacies

A Cook's Wares: 211 37th Street, Beaver Falls, PA 15010–2103, (412) 846–9490; utensils, knives, gadgets

Kitchen Etc.: 31 Lafayette Road, North Hampton, NH 03862, (800) 232–4070; discount kitchenware

Maid of Scandinavia: 3244 Raleigh Avenue, Minneapolis, MN 55416–2299, (612) 927–7996; baking supplies

Palanimals: P.O. Box 695, Kent, CT 06757, (203) 868–9206; bunny dolls

Primrose Cottage: White Oak Lane, Warren, CT 06754, (203) 868–0764; window cookie cutters

Wilton Enterprises Inc.: 2240 West 75th Street, Woodridge, IL 60517; cake decorating supplies

Bibliography

Bragdon, Allen D., Ed. *The Gingerbread Book*. New York: Arco Publishing, Inc., 1984

Gies, Joseph, and Frances Gies. *Life in a Medieval City*. New York: Harper & Row, 1968

Hieatt, Constance B., and Sharon Butler, Eds. *Curye on Inglysch*. Early English Text Society, 1985

Jarrett, Lauren, and Nancy Nagel. *Making and Baking Gingerbread Houses*. New York: Crown Publishers, Inc., 1984

Tournaments Illuminated, Society for Creative Anachronism, issue 97

Acknowledgments

I WOULD LIKE TO THANK my mom and dad, Joyce and Michael Johnson, for always expecting the best; Barbara Morgenroth for the words and encouragement; Barbara Hopefl for always keeping an eye out for new goodies; Ellen Prindle for her support; Richard Palan for his friendship and many hours; Barry and Carol O'Rourke for the use of their house; Naomi Warner for giving me the opportunity and Darilyn Lowe Carnes for all her hard work; The Warren Congregational Church; and my husband Kenny for believing in me.

T.J.L.

I would like to thank the staff of the New Milford Public Library for their research assistance; SueAnne Lawhorn Merrill, Corporate Minister of Arts & Sciences of the Society for Creative Anachronism, and Elizabeth of Dendermonde; Gert Trani, the assistant librarian at The Culinary Institute of America; Jan Murray of St. George's Church, Middlebury, CT; Fortune Pawlowski for her support; Robin and Sasha Morgenroth for their long and vivid memories; Ellen Rosefsky for her perspicacity; Madeline Anderson and her store Connecticut Memories for her generosity in supplying props; Sue Katz and Gareth Esersky for all they've done. And Teresa.

B.A.M.

Index